Edited by Jamie Bogner and Trish Faubion
Recipe development by Christopher Cina except pages 34, 36, 60, 76, 110, 116, 130, 134, and 150 by Sara Dumford.
Art direction and design by Jamie Bogner

Photography
Christopher Cina: Front cover and pages 9, 11, 13, 15, 19, 39, 41, 43, 44, 47, 55, 63, 65, 71, 75, 89, 99, 103, 125, 128, 133, 137, 139, 143, 149, 155, 157.
Matt Graves: Pages 6, 17, 21, 23, 25, 27, 29, 31, 33, 35, 37, 49, 51, 53, 57, 59, 61, 67, 69, 73, 77, 79, 81, 83, 85, 87, 90, 93, 95, 97, 101, 105, 107, 109, 111, 113, 115, 117, 119, 121, 123, 127, 131, 135, 141, 145, 147, 151, 153.

Unfiltered Media Group, LLC
214 S. College Ave., Ste. 3
Fort Collins, CO 80524
beerandbrewing.com

ISBN: 978-0-9962689-1-2 (Print); 978-0-9962689-5-0 (eBook)

Library of Congress Control Number: 2015919886

Printed in China through Asia Pacific Offset

10 9 8 7 6 5 4 3 2 1

THE BEST OF

Cooking
WITH
Beer

CRAFT **Beer**&**Brewing**

Contents

Starters & Small Bites   Page 7

APPETIZERS   PAGE 8
SIDES   PAGE 32

Lunches & Light Meals   Page 45

LIGHT & FUN   PAGE 46
SALADS   PAGE 60
SANDWICHES   PAGE 66
SOUPS & STEWS   PAGE 78

Suppers & Dinners   Page 91

FISH & SEAFOOD   PAGE 92
BEEF   PAGE 102
FOWL   PAGE 110
PORK   PAGE 116
BEANS & CHEESE   PAGE 124

Sweets & Desserts   Page 129

CAKES & COOKIES   PAGE 130
CHEESECAKES   PAGE 138
CUSTARDS, PUDDINGS & FROZEN DESSERT   PAGE 142
PIES & COBBLERS   PAGE 150
FUN SWEETS   PAGE 154

Index   Page 158

Legend

Throughout the book, we use these symbols:

 TIME

 INGREDIENTS

 BEER RECOMMENDATION

STARTERS &
SMALL BITES

ACTIVE PREP: 15 minutes
TOTAL TIME: 30 minutes
MAKES: 4 waffles

BROWN ALE WAFFLES
2 large eggs
1 cup (8 fl oz/237 ml) milk
⅔ cup (5.3 fl oz/157 ml) brown ale
⅓ cup (2.6 fl oz/77 ml) canola oil
2 cup all-purpose flour
1 Tbs baking powder
1 tsp kosher salt
Pan spray
8 oz (227 g) smoked salmon
½ cup red onion, julienned
1 recipe Toasted Capers
1 recipe Horseradish Crema
8 chive leaves

TOASTED CAPERS
1 Tbs butter
2 Tbs capers, drained

HORSERADISH CREMA
½ cup (4 fl oz/118 ml) sour cream
¼ cup (2 fl oz/59 ml) buttermilk
6 Tbs prepared horseradish
1 tsp kosher salt

Dogfish Head Brewery Palo Santo Marron
(MILTON, DELAWARE)
Surly Brewing Company Bender
(MINNEAPOLIS, MINNESOTA)
Avery Brewing Company Ellie's Brown Ale
(BOULDER, COLORADO)

Brown Ale Waffles with Smoked Salmon, Toasted Capers, Horseradish Crema

Preheat waffle iron.

Combine the eggs, milk, brown ale, and canola oil in a mixing bowl and mix well. In a separate bowl, combine the flour, baking powder, and salt and mix well. Add the dry ingredients to the wet ingredients and whisk until the batter is smooth. Spray the waffle iron, scoop 1 cup (8 fl oz/237 ml) of batter into the waffle iron, and cook following the directions for your waffle maker.

To assemble, separate each waffle into 3–4 pieces and layer each piece with the smoked salmon. Sprinkle the red onions and capers over each waffle. Spoon generous amounts of the Horseradish Crema over each waffle, garnish each waffle with 2 chive leaves, and serve.

Toasted Capers
Melt the butter in a small pan over medium-high heat. Add the capers and fry lightly in the butter until they are browned and crispy. Drain on paper towels.

Horseradish Crema
Combine all the ingredients and mix well.

ACTIVE PREP: 15 minutes
CURING TIME: 60–90 minutes
SERVES: 6–8

1 lb (454 g) raw shrimp, peeled and
  deveined
1 cup (8 fl oz/237 ml) fresh lime juice
  (about 5 limes)
½ cup (4 fl oz/118 ml) lager
1 tsp salt
1 cup Roma tomato, diced small
1 avocado, seeded and diced
1 jalapeño, minced
½ cup red onion, minced
½ bunch cilantro, chopped
1 tsp ground cumin, toasted
6 oz (170 g) crabmeat
¼ cup (2 fl oz/59 ml) olive oil

Victory Lager
(DOWNINGTOWN, PENNSYLVANIA)
Weihenstephaner Original
(FREISING, GERMANY)

If you're really adventurous, use a sour beer
with a citrusy *Brettanomyces* character
such as:

Crooked Stave Batch 100
(DENVER, COLORADO)
The Bruery Sour in the Rye
(PLACENTIA, CALIFORNIA)
Prairie Artisan Ales' Funky Gold Amarillo
(TULSA, OKLAHOMA)

Lager Citrus Cured Shrimp & Crab Ceviche

//

Cut the shrimp into quarters by first slicing in half lengthwise, then cross-wise. In a metal, nonreactive bowl, combine the shrimp, lime juice, beer, and salt. Mix well and chill for 60–90 minutes to cure the shrimp.

While the shrimp are curing, combine the remaining ingredients, mix well, and chill until needed.

The shrimp will be bright white and firm once cured. Drain the liquid from the shrimp, reserving ½ cup (4 fl oz/118 ml). Combine the vegetable-crab meat mixture with the shrimp, add the reserved curing liquid, and mix well.

Serve immediately with tortilla chips.

ACTIVE PREP: 10 minutes
MARINATING TIME: 48 hours
SERVES: 2–4

1 Tbs fresh parlsey, chopped
1½ Tbs fresh chives, minced
½ Tbs fresh rosemary, minced
1 Tbs fresh thyme, chopped
1 tsp garlic, minced
½ tsp salt
¼ tsp black pepper
½ cup (4 fl oz/118 ml) extra virgin olive oil
4 oz (113 g) Haystack Mountain goat
   cheese log, cut into 1-ounce (28 g) discs
Warm grilled bread

Victory Prima Pils
(DOWNINGTOWN, PENNSYLVANIA)
August Schell Pilsner
(NEW ULM, MINNESOTA)
Sixpoint The Crisp
(BROOKLYN, NEW YORK)
Ballast Point Pale Ale
(SAN DIEGO, CALIFORNIA)

Herb-Marinated Goat Cheese

Combine the parsley, chives, rosemary, thyme, garlic, salt, and pepper with the olive oil and mix well. Place the goat cheese discs into two 4-ounce (118 ml) resealable jars. Pour the herb oil over the cheese to cover. Seal the jar tightly and chill for 48 hours. Remove from the refrigerator and allow to warm to room temperature before spreading on the warm grilled bread.

ACTIVE PREP: 10 minutes
TOTAL TIME: 15 minutes
SERVES: 6–8

2 cup (16 fl oz/473 ml) Bock beer, chilled
1¾ cup (14 fl oz/414 ml) tomato juice, chilled
1 Tbs horseradish
1 Tbs Sriracha
1 tsp Worcestershire
1 Tbs (½ fl oz/15 ml) fresh lime juice
2 Tbs green onions, minced
1 pepperoncini, minced
1 tsp kosher salt
2 dozen East Coast oysters, shucked

Ayinger Celebrator
(AYING, GERMANY)
Epic Double Skull
(SALT LAKE CITY, UTAH)
Fort Collins Brewery Maibock
(FORT COLLINS, COLORADO)

Spicy Red Bock Beer Oyster "Shooters"

///

Combine the beer, tomato juice, horseradish, Sriracha, Worcestershire, lime juice, green onions, pepperoncini, and salt in a mixing bowl or pitcher and mix well.

Place an oyster in a shot glass. Top with about ¼ cup (1½–2 fl oz/44–59 ml) of "red beer." Serve cold.

ACTIVE PREP: 30 minutes
TOTAL TIME: 80 minutes
SERVES: 12

1 lb (454 g) ground lamb
½ cup onion, diced
1 egg
1 tsp cumin, ground
1 tsp salt
½ tsp black pepper, ground
⅓ cup panko bread crumbs
¼ cup chopped parsley
Ricotta salata

BEER-TOMATO BROTH
3 ripe tomatoes, roughly chopped
½ cup (4 fl oz/118 ml) amber ale
2 tsp salt
1 Tbs (½ fl oz/15 ml) olive oil
2 Tbs garlic, minced
1 pinch crushed red pepper
1 tsp thyme, chopped
1 green onion, sliced

New Belgium Fat Tire
(FORT COLLINS, COLORADO)
Ballast Point Calico Amber
(SAN DIEGO, CALIFORNIA)

Pair with:
Brasserie Dupont Saison Dupont
(TOURPES, BELGIUM)
Boulevard Saison Brett
(KANSAS CITY, MISSOURI)

Lamb Meatballs in Beer-Tomato Broth with Ricotta Salata

Ricotta salata is a variation of ricotta cheese that has been pressed, salted, and dried. It is hard and white and has a mildly salty, nutty, and milky flavor.

Preheat oven to 350°F (177°C). Combine all the ingredients except the ricotta salata in a mixing bowl and mix well. Roll the mixture into individual meatballs about the size of a walnut. Arrange on an oiled cookie sheet and bake until done (8–10 minutes).

Beer-Tomato Broth

Combine the tomatoes, beer, and 1 teaspoon of salt in a saucepan with a lid. Place on low heat and allow the tomatoes to soften and melt, 30–40 minutes. Strain the liquid through a fine mesh sieve and discard the solids.

In another saucepan, warm the oil over medium heat. Add the garlic, red pepper, and thyme and sweat slowly 2–3 minutes. Add the tomato liquid to the pan and reduce by one third. Season with the remaining 1 teaspoon of salt.

Place the meatballs in a bowl with a toothpick in each, top with a shaving of ricotta salata cut with a potato peeler, and add the tomato broth. Garnish with sliced green onion.

ACTIVE PREP: 5 minutes
TOTAL TIME: 20 minutes
SERVES: 4

BEER-POACHED SHRIMP
2 qt (64 fl oz/1.9 l) water
2 cup (16 fl oz/473 ml) IPA
½ lemon
2 Tbs salt
2 lb (907 g) shrimp

CURRIED MAYO
1 shallot, minced
1 cup (8 fl oz/237 ml) mayonnaise
1 Tbs curry powder
Juice of 1 lime
2 tsp salt

Try an English IPA such as:

Great Lakes Commodore Perry IPA
(CLEVELAND, OHIO)
Left Hand 400 Pound Monkey
(LONGMONT, COLORADO)
Yards IPA
(PHILADELPHIA, PENNSYLVANIA)
Samuel Smith's India Ale
(TADCASTER, U.K.)

IPA-Poached Shrimp with Curried Mayo Sauce

Beer-Poached Shrimp

In a large pot, bring the water, beer, and lemon to a boil. Add the salt, then the shrimp. Cook the shrimp until just opaque in the center, about 2 minutes. Drain and rinse under cold running water to cool. Peel and devein the shrimp, leaving the tails intact, if desired. Store covered in the refrigerator until ready to serve.

Curried Mayo

Combine all the ingredients in a bowl and mix well. Spoon into a small serving bowl and serve with the chilled Beer-Poached Shrimp.

ACTIVE PREP: 45 minutes
TOTAL TIME: 13 hours (including chilling the pork belly)
SERVES: 3–4

1 qt (32 fl oz/946 ml) apple cider
¼ cup (2 fl oz/59 ml) apple cider vinegar
2 lb (907 g) piece of pork belly, skin off and scored
1 onion, large dice
2 carrots, large dice
3 stalks celery, large dice
2 bay leaves
3 cup (24 fl oz/710 ml) IPA
2 cup (16 fl oz/473 ml) chicken stock
16 shallots
4 Tbs (1/2 stick) butter
2 apples, cored and cut into 12 equal pieces
12–16 wooden skewers, soaked in water
Kosher salt

Odell IPA
(FORT COLLINS, COLORADO)
Firestone Walker Union Jack
(PASO ROBLES, CALIFORNIA)

Crispy Pork Belly Skewers

Preheat oven to 325°F (163°C).

Combine the apple cider and cider vinegar in a saucepan and cook over medium-high heat to reduce to a syrup. Reserve this apple gastrique for the skewers.

In a large pan, sear the pork belly on both sides until golden brown. Place the pork belly in a baking pan with the onions, carrots, celery, bay leaf, IPA, and chicken stock. Cover and bake for 4 hours.

Remove the pork belly from the liquid to a second pan, place a third pan on top of the belly with 5 pounds (2.3 kg) of weight. Cooling the pork belly with the weight helps push out the excess fat and creates a leaner pork belly for the skewers. Refrigerate the weighted pork belly overnight.

To roast the shallots, melt the butter in an ovenproof pot over medium heat and add the shallots. Toss to cover the shallots in the butter. Place the pot in the oven and roast the shallots at 325°F (163°C) until soft and tender.

Once the pork belly has chilled, remove the excess fat and cut into 1-inch (2.5 cm) cubes.

Skewer 2 pieces of the pork belly with 2 pieces of apple and 2 shallots. Brown the skewers in a large pan over high heat or on a grill. Remove skewers to a plate and drizzle the apple gastrique over the skewers. Sprinkle with salt and serve.

ACTIVE PREP: 25 minutes
TOTAL TIME: 1 hour
SERVES: 4–6

12–15 large clams, cleaned
5 slices bacon, chopped
3 Tbs onion, minced
1 tsp minced garlic
2 Tbs chopped parsley
1 Tbs lemon juice
¼ cup (2 fl oz/59 ml) stout
1 cup panko bread crumbs
¼ cup grated Parmesan
Salt and freshly ground black pepper

Deschutes Obsidian Stout
(BEND, OREGON)
Alaskan Stout
(JUNEAU, ALASKA)
Newport Storm Winter Porter
(NEWPORT, RHODE ISLAND)

Rhode Island Stuffies

Stuffies (or stuffed clams, as they're called outside of Rhode Island) usually consist of a breadcrumb and minced clam mixture that is baked on the half shell of a quahog hard-shell clam. Beyond that basic foundation, there are as many different recipes as there are cooks. Some think that a stuffie should taste only of minced clams and clam-juice-soaked bread; some add chopped onion, celery, and peppers; some add sausage; some spice the mix with herbs such as sage, thyme, and oregano. Bacon, stout, and Parmesan give our version a savory, earthy twist.

Bring a large pot of water to a boil. Drop the clams into the boiling water and reduce the heat to low. Simmer until the clams have opened (about 6–8 minutes).

Remove the clams from the pot and allow to cool. Discard any clams with unopened shells.

Pull the meat from the shell avoiding the foot (the white muscle that holds the clam in place). Chop the clams finely. Twist the shells apart at the hinges and reserve.

Preheat the oven to 350°F (177°C). In a large sauté pan over medium-high heat, cook the bacon until it begins to brown. Reduce the heat to medium and add the onions. Cook until the onions become translucent, about 3–4 minutes. Add the garlic and cook for 1 minute. Add the parsley, chopped clams, lemon juice, and beer. Bring to a boil, then reduce heat to low.

When the liquid has reduced by half, add the bread crumbs. Stirring frequently, cook until the mixture has moistened to a stuffing consistency. Remove from the heat and allow the stuffing to cool. Fold in the Parmesan and season to taste with salt and black pepper.

Stuff the reserved clamshells with 2–3 tablespoons of the stuffing and bake for 20–25 minutes or until the stuffies begin to brown.

Remove from the oven and serve.

ACTIVE PREP: 1½ hours
TOTAL TIME: 3 hours
SERVES: 5–6

SUMMER SAUSAGE
1 lb (454 g) ground beef
2 lb (907 g) ground pork
3 Tbs kosher salt
2 tsp ground mustard seed or dry mustard
2 tsp garlic, chopped
2 tsp black pepper, crushed
½ Tbs sugar
4 tsp pink curing salt
1 Tbs smoked paprika
1 cup (8 fl oz/237 ml) ice cold pilsner
Hog casings (optional)

WHITE-BEER CHEDDAR DIJON
½ lb (227 g) white cheddar
1 tsp cornstarch
1½ cup (12 fl oz/355 ml) white beer
1 Tbs butter
2 Tbs (1 fl oz/30 ml) Dijon mustard

PICKLED ONIONS
½ cup (4 fl oz/118 ml) vinegar
1 cup (8 fl oz/237 ml) water
3 Tbs sugar
1 tsp salt
1 bay leaf
1 tsp black peppercorns
1 sprig thyme
1 red onion, sliced in thin rings

BISCUIT
3 cup cake flour
1 cup all-purpose flour
1 Tbs baking powder
2 tsp salt
1 tsp sugar
¼ lb (1 stick) butter, cut into pieces
2 Tbs solid vegetable shortening
2 cup (16 fl oz/473 ml) buttermilk
¼ cup (2 fl oz/59 ml) buttermilk and 1 egg yolk, mixed

Pilsner Urquell
(PILSEN, CZECH REPUBLIC)
Allagash White
(PORTLAND, MAINE)

Young Summer Sausage, White-Beer Cheddar Dijon, and Pickled Onion with a Buttermilk Biscuit

Summer Sausage

All ingredients should be as cold as you can get them without freezing. Mix all ingredients except the beer, in a stand mixer with a paddle. Add the beer to the mixture and emulsify the sausage. Test a teaspoon of the mix in simmering water to taste.

If you have access to hog casings and a sausage press, stuff the casings with the mixture. Otherwise, lay down a sheet of plastic wrap and place about 2 cups of the sausage mix in the middle of the sheet. Press the sausage into a log shape, and wrap the log in plastic pushing out as much air as possible. Repeat the process with plastic wrap and then foil.

Poach the cased or wrapped sausage in a 150°F (66°C) water bath for 20 minutes or until done. Cool, then remove the foil and plastic wrap and slice.

White-Beer Cheddar Dijon

Shred the cheese and toss it with the cornstarch in a bowl. Combine the beer and butter in a saucepan and bring them to a simmer. Turn off the heat and add the cheese mixture. Stirring constantly, bring the mixture back to the heat to thicken slightly. Add the mustard. Remove from the heat and puree in a blender on high.

Pickled Onions

Place the vinegar, water, sugar, salt, bay leaf, peppercorns, and thyme in a nonreactive saucepan and bring the mixture to a boil. Strain the mixture and add the onion rings. Let sit refrigerated until cool.

Biscuit

In a large bowl, combine the flour, baking powder, salt, and sugar. Add the butter and shortening to the dry ingredients and break up with your thumb and fingers until the mixture has a flaky texture. Add the buttermilk and stir together with a fork until the mixture just comes together. Do not overwork.

Roll out onto a floured surface. Cut out the biscuits with a 3-inch (7.6 cm) round cutter. Brush the biscuits with the buttermilk-egg-yolk mixture.

Bake at 400°F (204°C) until golden, about 10 minutes.

To serve, plate several sausage slices with a biscuit, pickled onions, and White-Beer Cheddar Dijon.

ACTIVE PREP: 20 minutes
TOTAL TIME: 90 minutes
SERVES: 4–6

3 cup (24 fl oz/710 ml) Pilsner
2 qt (64 fl oz/1.9 l) water
1 lb (454 g) shell-on medium shrimp
½ medium fennel bulb, thinly sliced
  (reserve the fronds)
½ medium onion, thinly sliced
2 cloves garlic, thinly sliced
½ Fresno chile or red jalapeño seeded and
  thinly sliced
½ cup (4 fl oz/118 ml) fresh lemon juice
¼ cup (2 fl oz/59 ml) apple cider vinegar
¼ cup (2 fl oz/59 ml) extra-virgin olive oil
2 Tbs reserved fennel fronds
Kosher salt
Freshly ground black pepper

Live Oak Pilz
(AUSTIN, TEXAS)
Firestone Walker Pivo Pils
(PASO ROBLES, CALIFORNIA)

Mason Jar Pickled Shrimp

//

Briny and spicy pickled shrimp are a staple of Southern cuisine. You can serve these after they've chilled for an hour, but the longer they sit in their pickle liquid, the better they get (up to about a week).

In a large pot, combine the beer and water. Bring to a boil. Add the shrimp and immediately turn off the heat. Let the pot with shrimp cool, untouched, for 10 minutes.

  Drain the shrimp and rinse them under cold running water to cool. Peel and devein the shrimp, leaving the tails intact, if desired. Combine the shrimp, fennel bulb, onion, garlic, chile, lemon juice, vinegar, oil, and fennel fronds in a medium bowl. Season with salt and pepper and toss to combine. Divide among 6–8 12 oz (355 ml) mason jars. Refrigerate for 1 hour and serve with crusty bread.

ACTIVE PREP: 40 minutes
TOTAL TIME: 24 hours
SERVES: 3–4

SRIRACHA CHICKEN WINGS
2 lb (907 kg) jumbo chicken wings
3½ cup (28 fl oz/828 ml) IPA, divided
1 Tbs salt
¾ cup (6 fl oz/177 ml) ketchup
½ cup (4 fl oz/118 ml) Sriracha sauce
1 Tbs (½ fl oz/15 ml) cider vinegar
2 Tbs (1 fl oz/30 ml) soy sauce
1 Tbs fresh ground ginger
1 Tbs cornstarch

BLUE CHEESE DIPPING SAUCE
1 cup blue cheese crumbles
½ cup (4 fl oz/118 ml) sour cream
¾ cup (6 fl oz/177 ml) mayonnaise
1 tsp Worcestershire
Salt and pepper

Thirsty Dog 330 Summit IPA
(AKRON, OHIO)

Also pairs well with your favorite fresh IPA
(or any beer you enjoy with hot wings)!

IPA Sriracha Chicken Wings with Blue Cheese Dipping Sauce

Sriracha Chicken Wings

Combine the chicken wings, 3 cup (24 fl oz/710 ml) IPA, and 1 tablespoon salt in a plastic container and refrigerate overnight.

Preheat the oven to 350°F (177°C). Drain the wings and lay them out on a sheet pan. Bake for 25 minutes, reversing the tray halfway through.

In a small saucepan, combine the remaining ½ cup (4 fl oz/118 ml) of IPA with the ketchup, Sriracha sauce, vinegar, soy sauce, ginger, and cornstarch. Bring to a simmer. When the wings are done, toss them with the sauce while hot.

For extra visual impact, quickly sear on a grill pan or grill to add visible grill marks.

Blue Cheese Dipping Sauce

Combine the blue cheese, sour cream, mayonnaise, and Worcestershire in bowl and mix until combined. Season to taste with salt and pepper.

ACTIVE PREP: 10 minutes
TOTAL TIME: 1 hour 10 minutes
SERVES: 1–2

1 cup (8 fl oz/237 ml) red/brown sour beer
¼ cup (2 fl oz/59 ml) rice wine vinegar
¼ cup (2 fl oz/59 ml) soy sauce
½ cup shallots, minced
1 Tbs ground black pepper
1 dozen Pacific oysters, shucked in the
  shell

New Belgium La Folie
(FORT COLLINS, COLORADO)
The Rare Barrel Another World
(BERKELEY, CALIFORNIA)
Rodenbach Grand Cru
(ROESELARE, BELGIUM)

Pacific Oysters with Sour Beer Mignonette

Traditionally served with raw oysters, mignonette sauce is usually made with minced shallots, cracked pepper, and vinegar. Here, we've substituted sour beer for some of the vinegar and added a little soy sauce.

In a small mixing bowl, combine the beer, vinegar, soy sauce, shallots, and ground pepper. Mix well. Refrigerate for 1 hour.

To serve, top each oyster with 1 tablespoon (½ fl oz/15 ml) mignonette.

ACTIVE PREP: 5 minutes
TOTAL TIME: 15 minutes
SERVES: 4

Oil for frying
1 cup cornmeal, fine ground
½ cup self-rising flour
1 tsp sugar
Pinch garlic powder
1 tsp kosher salt
Pinch cayenne pepper
1 egg
½ cup (4 fl oz/118 ml) ESB ale
½ cup onion, diced small
1 jalapeño (seeds removed), minced

Left Hand Brewing Sawtooth Ale
(LONGMONT, COLORADO)
Green Man ESB
(ASHEVILLE, NORTH CAROLINA)

ESB Hush Puppies

Don't toss these hush puppies to dogs to quell their barking! The beer isn't good for them, and these ESB-spiked morsels are certainly too tasty to waste!

In a deep fryer, heat 2–3 inches (5–8 cm) of oil to 350°F (177°C). In a medium bowl, combine the cornmeal, flour, sugar, garlic powder, salt, and cayenne. In a separate bowl combine the egg, beer, onion, and jalapeño and mix well. Pour the wet mixture over the dry mixture and stir together until well combined. Drop tablespoon-size mounds of batter into the oil, making sure to not crowd the pan. Cook, flipping halfway through, until the hush puppies are golden brown (3–4 minutes).

ACTIVE PREP: 10 minutes
TOTAL TIME: 45 minutes
SERVES: 4

1 lb (454 g) Brussels sprouts
1 Tbs (½ fl oz/15 ml) olive oil
½ tsp salt
¼ tsp pepper
1 large garlic clove, minced
2 shallots, peeled and sliced
1/8 tsp chili flakes
½ cup (4 fl oz/118 ml) Belgian ale

Make with:
Ommegang Tripel Perfection
(COOPERSTOWN, NEW YORK)

Pair with:
Firestone Walker Union Jack IPA
(PASO ROBLES, CALIFORNIA)

Spicy Belgian Ale Brussels

//

Preheat the oven to 375°F (190°C).

Wash the Brussels sprouts. Trim the root end and cut each Brussels sprout in half lengthwise, keeping the root end intact. In a medium bowl, toss the Brussels sprouts with the oil, salt, pepper, garlic, shallots, and chili flakes. Transfer to a 5" × 8" (13 cm × 20 cm) baking pan, and pour the beer around the Brussels sprouts. Roast 30–35 minutes, until nicely browned, crisp on the outside and tender. Season with salt and pepper to taste and serve.

ACTIVE PREP: 30 minutes
TOTAL TIME: 2½ hours
SERVES: 6–8 as a snack with beer

VEGETABLES

2 medium carrots, cut into 4" (10 cm) sticks,
¼" (6 mm) wide

8 oz (227 g) pickling cucumbers, cut into
6 wedges lengthwise

1 red pepper, cut into 4" (10 cm) sticks, ¼"
(6 mm) wide

1 yellow pepper, cut into 4" (10 cm) sticks,
¼" (6 mm) wide

PICKLING LIQUID

2 cup (16 fl oz/473 ml) sour beer

½ cup (4 fl oz/118 ml) white wine vinegar

3 Tbs sugar

1 Tbs salt (Pickling salt is best, but
kosher salt will work.*)

2 Tbs mustard seed (a mix
of black and yellow is nice)

2 tsp coriander seeds

1 tsp black peppercorn

2 whole bay leaves

4 garlic cloves, peeled and smashed

Pinch of crushed red pepper

The Bruery Sour in the Rye
(PLACENTIA, CALIFORNIA)

Quick Sour Beer Pickled Vegetables

Place the cut vegetables into a heat-proof bowl. Separately, combine the pickling liquid ingredients in a medium saucepan over medium-high heat. Bring the liquid to a boil, then reduce to a simmer. Simmer for 5 minutes to dissolve the sugar and salt. Pour the hot liquid over the vegetables and stir. Chill the vegetables for at least 2 hours, stirring occasionally. Serve. Store leftovers in the refrigerator for up to 7 days.

*Kosher or iodized salt may turn the brining liquid cloudy.

ACTIVE PREP: 25 minutes
TOTAL TIME: 25 minutes
SERVES: 2

2 portobello mushrooms
3–4 cup ((24–32 fl oz/710–946 ml) oil
  for frying
Salt and pepper to taste

BATTER
2 cup all-purpose flour
¼ cup cornstarch
1 cup (8 fl oz/237 ml) lager (maybe a tad
  more)
1 shot (1.5 fl oz/44 ml) whiskey
1 tsp salt

GRIBICHE SAUCE
3 eggs boiled, shelled, and chopped
1 dill pickle, finely chopped
½ bunch parsley, finely chopped
1 Tbs capers, chopped
1 cup (8 fl oz/237 ml) mayonnaise
½ cup (4 fl oz/118 ml) ketchup
1 Tbs tarragon, chopped
Juice of one lemon

For the batter:
Samuel Adams Boston Lager
(BOSTON, MASSACHUSETTS)

Pair with a brown ale such as:
Big Sky's Moose Drool
(MISSOULA, MONTANA)
Surly Bender
(MINNEAPOLIS, MINNESOTA)

Boiler Maker Battered Portobello Fries with Gribiche Sauce

Portobello Fries

In a medium bowl, combine all the ingredients. With a wire whisk, whip until smooth.

With a spoon, scrape the gills from the mushrooms. Cut the caps into ½-inch (13 mm) strips. Heat a wok or deep fryer to 375°F (191°C). Dunk the portobellos in the batter and fry until lovely. Season with salt and pepper directly out of the fryer.

Gribiche Sauce

In a small bowl, combine all the ingredients and mix well. Serve with Portobello fries.

ACTIVE PREP: 35 minutes
TOTAL TIME: 70 minutes
MAKES: 20–24 fritters

1 head cauliflower
Kosher salt
4 slices bacon
3 large eggs
1 Tbs minced garlic
2 Tbs chopped parsley
4 oz (113 g) Gruyère, shredded
½ cup (4 fl oz/118 ml) Vienna lager
5 Tbs flour
1 tsp baking powder
4 Tbs butter

Samuel Adams Boston Lager
(BOSTON, MASSACHUSETTS)
Devils Backbone Brewing Vienna Lager
(ROSELAND, VIRGINIA)
Great Lakes Brewing Company Eliot Ness
(CLEVELAND, OHIO)

Cauliflower-Bacon Fritters

Cut the cauliflower into florets and place into a pot of water with ½ tablespoon salt. Bring to a simmer and cook for 15 minutes or until the cauliflower is fork tender. Remove the cauliflower from the heat, drain, and allow to cool to room temperature.

Cook the bacon until crispy, allow to cool, and chop.

In a large mixing bowl, combine the eggs, garlic, parsley, chopped bacon, Gruyère, Vienna lager, and 1 tablespoon salt. Using a fork, mash the cauliflower into small pieces and add to the mixing bowl, mixing well.

Add the flour and baking powder, mix well and chill for 30 minutes.

In a large sauté pan, melt the butter over medium-high heat. Spoon golf-ball size dollops of batter into the pan and flatten with the back of the spoon. Brown the fritter, flip and brown the other side 4–5 minutes. Remove from the pan and drain on paper towels. Serve warm.

You can omit the bacon from this recipe to keep it vegetarian.

ACTIVE PREP: 20 minutes

TOTAL TIME: 13–15 hours (including the crème fraiche)

SERVES: 3–4

POTATO SKINS

3 Russet potatoes, scrubbed

¼ cup (2 fl oz/59 ml) olive oil

2 tsp kosher salt, divided

6 oz (170 g) pancetta, cooked crispy and chopped

8 oz (227 g) Comté cheese, shredded

½ cup chives, sliced

½ cup (4 fl oz/118 ml) crème fraiche (see below)

Freshly cracked black pepper

CRÈME FRAICHE

2 cup (16 fl oz/473 ml) heavy cream

2 Tbs (1 fl oz/30 ml) buttermilk

Pair with an English-style pale or mild: Summit Brewing Union Series 3X Mild **(ST. PAUL, MINNESOTA)**

Grown-Up Potato Skins

///

Preheat the oven to 400ºF (204°C). Rub the potatoes with the olive oil and 1 tsp of the salt. Place in the oven and bake for 70 minutes or until potatoes are tender on the inside and skin begins to crisp. Remove the potatoes from the oven and allow them to cool until you can handle them.

Halve the potatoes and, using a spoon, scoop out the potato flesh being careful to leave ¼-inch to ½ inch (6–13 mm) of potato on the bottom. Reserve the potato flesh for another use. Place the potato skins in a pan and top with the pancetta and Comté. Broil under high heat until the cheese has melted and the potato begins to brown. Remove from the oven and finish with a dollop of crème fraiche and a sprinkle of chives on each potato. Sprinkle with the remaining salt and freshly cracked black pepper.

To turn this dish into a meal, combine blanched broccoli with the reserved potato flesh and fill the potato skins before you broil them.

Crème Fraiche

Combine the cream and buttermilk in a nonreactive container. Cover with a clean towel and place in a warm area. Let sit for 12–14 hours. Refrigerate.

LUNCHES & LIGHT MEALS

ACTIVE PREP: 45 minutes
TOTAL TIME: 1 hour
SERVES: 4

CARAMELIZED SWEET POTATOES
2 cup sweet potatoes, peeled and diced
2 Tbs butter
¼ cup (2 fl oz/59 ml) Doppelbock

DOPPELBOCK-FIG DRESSING
1 small shallot, chopped
1 clove garlic
3–4 fresh figs, stemmed
2 Tbs (1 fl oz/30 ml) Doppelbock
4 Tbs (2 fl oz/59 ml) balsamic vinegar
2 Tbs (1 fl oz/30 ml) olive oil
2 Tbs (1 fl oz/30 ml) canola oil
Kosher salt
Black pepper

PANZANELLA SALAD
Two 7–8 oz (198–227 g) duck breasts
1 tsp olive oil
2 cup dried bread cubes from an Italian loaf
2 cup Caramelized Sweet Potatoes
1 recipe Doppelbock-Fig Dressing
2 cup baby lettuce mix
½ cup walnut pieces, toasted
3 oz (85 g) goat cheese, crumbled
2 oz (57 g) prosciutto or ham, julienned
Kosher salt
Black pepper

Epic Brewing Company Double Skull
(SALT LAKE CITY, UTAH)
Jack's Abby Brewing Saxonator
(FRAMINGHAM, MASSACHUSETTS)
Ayinger Brewery Celebrator
(AYING, GERMANY)

Seared Duck Breast with Caramelized Sweet Potato Panzanella, Doppelbock-Fig Dressing

Caramelized Sweet Potatoes
Preheat oven to 350°F (177°C). In a cast-iron pan, melt the butter over medium heat, add the sweet potatoes, and cook until the butter begins to crackle. Mix the sweet potatoes in the pan to make sure they are covered in butter. Deglaze with the Doppelbock and place in the oven for 15 minutes.

Doppelbock-Fig Dressing
In a blender, combine the shallot, garlic, figs, Doppelbock, vinegar, and oils. Puree till smooth. Season with salt and pepper. Preheat oven to 350° (177°C).

Panzanella Salad
Score the skin side of the duck breast, making sure not to go into the meat below the skin. In a medium-size pan, add the olive oil and place on medium heat. When hot, add the duck breasts to the pan skin side down. Allow the skin to render slowly, getting crispy and golden brown. Sprinkle a little salt on the meat and turn over. Place the pan in the oven and cook 5–6 more minutes to cook the duck to medium, a little less if you prefer the duck closer to medium rare.

Remove the duck from the oven, take the duck out of the pan and place on a clean cutting board. Pour the drippings from the pan into a large mixing bowl. Add the bread cubes, Caramelized Sweet Potatoes, Doppelbock-Fig Dressing, baby lettuce, walnuts, goat cheese, and prosciutto to the mixing bowl and mix well. Season with salt and pepper. Allow this Panzanella salad to sit while you slice the duck thinly. Arrange the duck slices on 4 plates, top with the Panzanella salad, and serve.

ACTIVE PREP: 60 minutes
TOTAL TIME: 3 hours
SERVES: 4

TOMATILLO SALSA

1 lb (454 g) tomatillos, papery skin removed
    and rinsed
¼ cup (2 fl oz/59 ml) olive oil, plus
    additional to coat the tomatillos
¼ lb (113 g) yellow onion, diced small
5 cloves garlic
¼ cup (2 fl oz/59 ml) lime juice
½ cup (4 fl oz/118 ml) Vienna lager
½ bunch cilantro, leaves only
½ tsp ground cumin seed
1 tsp dark chili powder
1 tsp kosher salt or to taste

ALAMOSA STRIPED BASS

1 side Alamosa striped bass or other mild-fla-
    vored fish (1½–2 lb/680–907 g)
1 tsp olive oil
Salt and pepper
2 Tbs (1 fl oz/30 ml) grapeseed oil

TOSTADAS

2 cup (16 fl oz/473 ml) grapeseed oil
8 small white corn tortillas
1 tsp kosher salt
½ red onion, diced
1 handful cilantro, chopped
2 green onions, thinly sliced on the bias
½ lime, cut in wedges
1 tsp kosher salt

Devils Backbone Vienna Lager
(ROSELAND, VIRGINIA)
August Schell Firebrick
(NEW ULM, MINNESOTA)
Live Oak Big Bark Amber
(AUSTIN, TEXAS)

Alamosa Striped Bass Tostadas with Lager Tomatillo Salsa

Alamosa Striped Bass is a hybrid striped bass (a cross between the striped bass and the white bass) farmed in Alamosa, Colorado, by a family-owned company, Colorado Catch. It is a moderately fatty and mild-tasting fish with a firm, yet flaky texture. Well-suited to a variety of cuisines, here it is paired with tomatillos and Vienna lager to upscale the traditional tostada.

Tomatillo Salsa

Preheat the broiler. Halve the tomatillos, toss with olive oil to coat, and spread them skin side up on a sheet pan. Broil them for 5–7 minutes, until the skins begin to blister and blacken and they start to release their liquid. Remove from the oven and cool to room temperature.

Combine the tomatillos and their liquid with the ¼ cup (2 fl oz/59 ml) of olive oil and remaining ingredients, except the salt. Purée with a hand blender or in a food processor. Season to taste with salt and chill for at least 2 hours before serving.

Alamosa Striped Bass

Clean the fish from head to tail, trimming the fat off the belly and removing the bones (or have your fishmonger do this for you). Coat the fish with olive oil and season to taste with salt and pepper.

In a large sauté pan over medium to high heat, add the grapeseed oil and heat for 1–2 minutes, until the oil is hot. Place the fish skin side down and cook 4–5 minutes on each side. Remove the fish from the pan and place skin side down on paper towels to drain. When drained and cooled slightly, flake the fish with a fork to pull it off the skin. Reserve.

Tostadas

In a large pan with high sides, heat the grapeseed oil to 325°F (163°C). Fry the tortillas for 2–3 minutes on each side, until they are light golden brown and crispy (they will start to bubble when they are done). Remove from the oil and place on paper towels to drain. Season to taste with salt while they are still hot.

To serve, divide the flaked fish evenly among the tortillas and top with the Tomatillo Salsa and red onion, cilantro, and scallions. Season with a squeeze of lime and salt to taste.

ACTIVE PREP: 20 minutes
TOTAL TIME: 1½ hours
MAKES: About 16 crab cakes

1 lemon, zested and juiced
¼ cup parlsey, chopped
2 oz (57 g) red bell pepper, finely diced
¼ cup capers, drained and chopped
2 oz (57 g) shallots, minced
2 eggs
1 egg yolk
6 Tbs (3 fl oz/89 ml) IPA
½ cup (4 fl oz/118 ml) mayonnaise
1½ tsp kosher salt
Pinch of cayenne pepper
1 tsp dry mustard, ground
1 tsp Old Bay Seasoning
2 lb (907 g) rock crabmeat, drained
1 lb (454 g) jumbo lump crabmeat, drained
1 oz (28 g) panko bread crumbs
4–6 Tbs (2–3 fl oz/59–89 ml) canola oil

Uinta Hop Nosh
(SALT LAKE CITY, UTAH)
Union Craft Beer Double Duckpin
(BALTIMORE, MARYLAND)

Maryland Beer Crab Cakes

///

If you like crab cakes, you will love this classic recipe featuring fresh rock and lump crabmeat that is seasoned with IPA and—of course—Old Bay Seasoning.

Combine the lemon zest and juice, parsley, red pepper, capers, shallots, eggs and yolk, beer, capers, mayonnaise, salt, cayenne pepper, ground mustard, Old Bay Seasoning, and mix well. Gently fold in the crabmeat taking care not to break up the crab too much. Fold in the panko bread crumbs and mix gently. Chill for 1 hour.

In a large nonstick pan over medium-high heat, heat the oil. Form the crab mix into 3–4 ounce (85–113 g) patties and place in the pan gently. When the patties are browned on the bottom, carefully flip them. Serve the crab cakes with tartar sauce, or for a traditional Baltimore touch, serve with a lemon wedge and saltine crackers.

ACTIVE PREP: 60 minutes
TOTAL TIME: 1¼ hours
SERVES: 4

2 cup goat cheese
½ cup (4 fl oz/118 ml) lambic, gueuze,
  or other sour beer
2 Tbs basil chiffonade
Pinch of salt
4 poblano peppers
Cooking oil
4 eggs, lightly beaten
2 cup all-purpose flour
3 cup semolina

The Rare Barrel Forces Unseen
(BERKELEY, CALIFORNIA)
Crooked Stave Flor D'Lees
(DENVER, COLORADO)
Boon Oude Gueuze
(LEMBEEK, BELGIUM)

Sour Beer Goat Cheese Chile Rellenos

Here we pair tangy goat cheese with sour beer and basil for an intriguing and tart, earthy filling for these chile rellenos. There are a number of ways to char the peppers, from charcoal grill to gas grill or even a butane torch. The process of slitting, stuffing, and frying chile rellenos takes some practice, but it's worth it. And even the less-than-perfect ones are delicious.

In a mixing bowl, combine the goat cheese, beer, basil, and salt. Mix well and set aside.

Preheat the grill to high. Lightly rub the poblano peppers with the cooking oil. Fill a mixing bowl with ice water. Place the peppers on the grill and char the skin on each side. (This can also be done in an oven at a high temperature.)

When the skin has sufficiently blackened around the peppers, remove them from the heat and place them in the ice water to stop the cooking. When the peppers are cool, carefully remove the skin with your fingers or by scraping with a paring knife, making sure not to cut the skin. Ideally, the peppers should be left intact, but if not, it's not that big of a deal.

Once you've removed the charred skin, with a sharp knife make a cut in the pepper from the top to the bottom, just enough for you to scrape out the seeds. Divide the goat cheese into 4 pieces to match the size of the peppers. (Peppers may vary in size, but each should average about a ½ cup of your goat cheese mixture.) With your hands, roll the goat cheese into an oblong shape and slide each oblong piece inside a pepper. Press the cut edges of the peppers together and refrigerate for 30 minutes to allow the cheese to firm up.

Line up, in three separate pans, your breading ingredients: flour, then egg, then semolina. Roll each pepper in the flour first, coating well and knocking off any extra flour. Dip the floured pepper in the egg mixture, shake off any excess, and then roll the pepper in the semolina. You can keep these prepared rellenos in the refrigerator for up to 3 days before the next step.

Preheat a deep fryer to 350°F (177°C). Fry the peppers until they become golden brown, 2–3 minutes. Serve hot with a black bean sauce.

ACTIVE PREP: 25 minutes
TOTAL TIME: 1½ hours
SERVES: 4

QUICHE CRUST (PÂTE BRISÉE)

2½ cup flour

1 tsp salt

1 Tbs sugar

1 cup (2 sticks) butter, cut into pieces and chilled

½ cup (4 fl oz/118 ml) ice water

FILLING

6 oz (170 g) bacon, cooked and chopped

4 oz (113 g) cheddar, shredded

½ cup red onion, julienned

4 eggs

1 cup (8 fl oz/237 ml) pale ale

1 cup (8 fl oz/237 ml) half-and-half

Salt

Odell 5 Barrel Pale Ale
(FORT COLLINS, COLORADO)
Firestone Walker DBA
(PASO ROBLES, CALIFORNIA)

Pale Ale Bacon, Cheddar, and Onion Quiche

Quiche Crust (Pâte Brisée)

In a food processor, combine the flour, salt, and sugar and mix well. Add the chilled butter and process until the dough looks mealy. A little at a time, add chilled water until the dough just comes together. Remove from the processor, cover and allow to rest in the refrigerator for 30 minutes.

Remove the dough from the refrigerator to a floured work surface. Roll the dough to about ⅙-inch (4 mm) thick and lay into a 9-inch (23 cm) pie pan.

Filling

Preheat oven to 325°F (163°C). Arrange the bacon, cheddar, and onion evenly over the quiche crust. In a mixing bowl, combine the eggs, beer, half-and-half, and a pinch of salt. Pour the mixture over the bacon, cheddar, and onion. Bake for 30–35 minutes, until the quiche is set.

ACTIVE PREP: 40 minutes
TOTAL TIME: 1¼ hours
SERVES: 4

SAUTÉED MUSHROOMS

2 Tbs (1 fl oz/30 ml) olive oil

1 Tbs garlic, minced

2 lb (907 g) wild mushrooms (crimini, shiitake, oyster, maitake, black trumpet, chanterelle, morel and/or any combination of the above), cleaned

½ cup (4 fl oz/118 ml) white wine

2 cup (16 fl oz/473 ml) American strong ale

2 Tbs unsalted butter

Salt and black pepper

HERBED POLENTA

3½ cup (28 fl oz/828 ml) water

½ cup (4 fl oz/118 ml) milk

2 cup (16 fl oz/473 ml) American strong ale

4 Tbs butter

2 cup polenta, dry (not quick cooking)

1 Tbs rosemary, chopped

1 Tbs thyme, chopped

2 Tbs parsley, chopped

1 cup Parmesan, grated

Salt and freshly ground black pepper

Southern Tier Gemini
(LAKEWOOD, NEW YORK)
The Lost Abbey Deliverance
(SAN MARCOS, CALIFORNIA)

Beer-Braised Mushrooms with Herbed Polenta

//

American strong ale adds an intriguing layer to this flavorful dish. Serve it as a light lunch or as an appetizer.

Sautéed Mushrooms

In a sauté pan over medium heat, heat the oil and the garlic. Sweat the garlic for about 10 seconds. Add the mushrooms and sauté until the water is released. Deglaze the pan with the white wine and cook until the white wine has evaporated. Add the beer and cook until only a few tablespoons of beer remain. Remove from the heat and add the butter. Stir until the butter has melted. Season to taste with salt and pepper.

Herbed Polenta

Combine the water, milk, beer, and butter in a large saucepan and bring to a boil over medium heat. Whisk in the polenta and stir until the mixture begins to thicken. Add the herbs. Reduce the heat to medium, cover, and cook 40 minutes, stirring frequently. Stir in the Parmesan and mix until the Parmesan melts. Season to taste with salt and pepper. Spoon the hot polenta into a serving bowl and top with the sautéed mushrooms.

ACTIVE PREP: 40 minutes
TOTAL TIME: 1 hour
SERVES: 2–3

SPAETZLE
1 cup all-purpose flour
½ tsp nutmeg
¼ tsp white pepper
½ tsp salt
¼ cup (2 fl oz/59 ml) milk
2 eggs
2 Tbs (1 fl oz/30 ml) olive oil
2 Tbs butter for sautéing

CHEESE SAUCE
½ lb (227 g) fontina
1 Tbs cornstarch
1 cup (8 fl oz/237 ml) Belgian golden
   strong ale
1 Tbs butter

Brouwerij Huyghe Delirium Tremens
(MELLE, BELGIUM)
The Bruery Mischief
(PLACENTIA, CALIFORNIA)

Fontina Spaetzle and Cheese

This twist on the classic mac-and-cheese gets an extra boost from Belgian-style golden strong ale.

Spaetzle

In a medium bowl, combine the flour, nutmeg, and pepper. Mix well. In a separate bowl, beat the milk and eggs together. Add the wet ingredients to the dry ingredients and mix until well combined.

Bring to boil a gallon (128 fl oz/3.8 l) of salted water. Working in batches, with a rubber spatula, push the dough through an inverted flat cheese grater into the boiling water. Scoop out the spaetzle when it floats to the top. Drop it into a bowl of ice water to stop the cooking. Drain the water from the spaetzle. Toss the spaetzle in the olive oil to hold just as you would for pasta.

Cheese Sauce

Cube the cheese and toss it with the cornstarch. In a small saucepan, bring the beer to a simmer and add the butter. Turn off the heat and add the cheese to the beer stirring constantly until it comes together.

Place the mix in a blender and puree until creamy smooth.

In a nonstick or well-seasoned pan, sauté the spaetzle in the 2 tablespoons of butter until crispy and golden brown. Combine the spaetzle and cheese sauce. Garnish with a little lemon juice and parsley leaves or toasted bread crumbs.

ACTIVE PREP: 20 minutes
TOTAL TIME: 30 minutes
SERVES: 8–10

GRUIT PESTO DRESSING

½ cup (4 fl oz/118 ml) gruit
2–3 garlic cloves, peeled and chopped
1 cup basil leaves, packed
½ cup parsley, coarse stems removed, packed
2 oz (57 g) freshly grated Parmesan cheese
½ cup (4 fl oz/118 ml) extra virgin olive oil
¾ tsp salt
Freshly ground black pepper, as needed

SALAD

1 cup mini farfalle or ditalini pasta
1 recipe Gruit Pesto Dressing
1 head romaine lettuce, chopped
1 cup grape tomatoes, halved
1 zucchini, diced
1 yellow pepper, diced
1 cup jarred marinated artichokes, drained and chopped
½ cup brine-cured olives (such as Kalamata or Manzanilla)
8 oz (227 g) Italian salami, diced
8 oz (227 g) provolone cheese, diced
¼ cup fresh basil, cut into thin strips
Freshly ground black pepper

New Belgium Brewing Lips of Faith Gruit
(FORT COLLINS, COLORADO)
Founders Brewing Company Gruit
(GRAND RAPIDS, MICHIGAN)

Chopped Salad with Gruit Pesto Dressing

Gruit Pesto Dressing

Add the gruit, garlic, basil, parsley, and Parmesan cheese to a food processor or blender. With motor running, slowly add the olive oil and puree until smooth. Season to taste with salt and pepper.

Salad

Cook the pasta per package instructions. Drain and while hot, toss with ½ cup (4 fl oz/118 ml) of the Gruit Pesto Dressing. Set aside to cool slightly.

Combine the lettuce, vegetables, artichoke hearts, olives, salami, and cheese in a serving bowl. Toss generously with the ½ cup (4 fl oz/118 ml) of the Gruit Pesto Dressing. Add the pasta and basil to the mixture, toss, and top with additional Gruit Pesto Dressing and freshly ground black pepper as desired.

ACTIVE PREP: 30 minutes
TOTAL TIME: 35 minutes
SERVES: 4

BEER BARLEY
6 cup (48 fl oz/1.4 l) water
2 cup (16 fl oz/473 ml) IPA
1 lb (454 g) barley, rinsed
1 lemon, halved
1 Tbs minced garlic
2 bay leaves
Pinch crushed red pepper
2 Tbs salt

BLUE CHEESE VINAIGRETTE
2 shallots, peeled and minced
1 cup (8 fl oz/237 ml) champagne vinegar
2 Tbs (1 fl oz/30 ml) smooth Dijon mustard
1 lb (454 g) crumbled blue cheese
2 cup (16 fl oz/473 ml) canola oil
1 cup (8 fl oz/237 ml) olive oil
1 bunch parsley, chopped
Kosher salt
Black pepper

SALAD
1 lb (454 g) broccoli, charred on the grill
1 sweet potato, peeled, diced, and boiled until tender
1 cup walnuts, toasted
8 oz (227 g) baby lettuces mix
1 lb (454 g) Beer Barley, cooled
1–1½ cup (8–12 fl oz/237–355 ml) Blue Cheese Vinaigrette
Blue cheese to garnish
Black pepper

Barley Brown's Pallet Jack
(BAKER CITY, OREGON)
10 Barrel Joe IPA
(BEND, OREGON)

Charred Broccoli and Beer-Barley Salad with Blue Cheese Vinaigrette

Barley cooked in IPA adds a nutty, rustic element to this salad with charred broccoli and sweet potato.

Beer Barley

In a medium saucepan, bring the water and beer to a boil. Add the remaining ingredients and cook until the barley is tender, about 25 minutes. Remove the lemon and the bay leaves and strain the barley. Reserve at room temperature until you assemble your salad.

Blue Cheese Vinaigrette

In a medium bowl, combine the shallots and vinegar and let sit for 5 minutes. Add the Dijon mustard and stir well. Add half of the blue cheese, mixing well.

Slowly whisk in the oils until fully incorporated. Add the remaining blue cheese and mix well. Add parsley and season to taste with salt and pepper.

Salad

Toss all the ingredients in a large mixing bowl and divide among four plates. Garnish with crumbled blue cheese and freshly ground black pepper.

ACTIVE PREP: 15 minutes
TOTAL TIME: 3½ hours
SERVES: 3–4

PANZANELLA

1 loaf French or Italian bread
1 cup (8 fl oz/237 ml) canola oil
6 slices salami, cut into quarters
¼ cup Kalamata olives, roughly chopped
½ cup Gouda cheese, shredded
1 cup fennel, julienned
1 head Boston Bibb lettuce, washed,
    halved, core removed, and leaves torn
    into large pieces
1 tsp fresh thyme leaves
16 leaves parsley
¼ cup (2 fl oz/59 ml) Belgian trippel
4–6 oz Creamy Dressing (recipe below)

CREAMY DRESSING

½ cup (4 fl oz/118 ml) red wine vinegar
2 Tbs 1 fl oz/29 ml) Dijon mustard
1 cup (8 fl oz/237 ml) olive oil
1 cup (8 fl oz/237 ml) canola oil
1 Tbs fresh thyme leaves
¾ cup (6 fl oz/177 ml) mayonnaise
Salt and freshly ground black pepper

Brouwerij Bosteels Tripel Karmeliet
(BUGGENHOUT, BELGIUM)
Chimay White
(CHIMAY, BELGIUM)
Smuttynose Tripel
(HAMPTON, NEW HAMPSHIRE)

Fennel-Olive Panzanella with Gouda and Crispy Salami

Panzanella

Preheat the oven to 170°F (77°C). Tear the bread into large chunks, about the size of a golf ball. Place the bread onto a sheet pan and bake for 2–3 hours, or until the bread is dry and crispy (it shouldn't get brown).

In a large sauté pan over medium-high heat, heat the canola oil. Gently fry the salami in the oil until the bubbles are almost gone. Remove the salami to a paper towel to drain and cool. (When you remove the salami, it will still be soft, but it will crisp as it cools.)

In a large bowl, toss together the remaining ingredients and the cooled salami. To give the bread time to absorb some of the beer and dressing, let the salad rest for 5 minutes before serving. Season to taste with salt and freshly cracked black pepper.

Creamy Dressing

In a medium bowl, whisk together the vinegar and mustard. Slowly whisk in the olive and canola oils until the oils are fully incorporated and emulsified. Whisk in the thyme leaves and mayonnaise. Season to taste with salt and pepper.

ACTIVE PREP: 35 minutes
TOTAL TIME: 55 minutes
SERVES: 2

BROWN BEER MORNAY SAUCE

1½ cup (12 fl oz/355 ml) milk

4 Tbs butter

4 Tbs flour

1 cup (8 fl oz/237 ml) brown ale, room temperature

1 shallot, finely chopped

Pinch nutmeg

4 oz (113 g) Gruyère, shredded

Salt

SANDWICH

2 slices Pullman Loaf, sliced 1" (2.5 cm) thick

8 oz (227 g) turkey, sliced

4 slices bacon, cooked crispy

4 slices ripe tomato

1½ cup (12 fl oz/355 ml) Brown Beer Mornay Sauce

Fresh cracked black pepper

Uinta Bristlecone
(SALT LAKE CITY, UTAH)
Against the Grain The Brown Note
(LOUISVILLE, KENTUCKY)
Port Brewing Board Meeting
(SAN MARCOS, CALIFORNIA)

Kentucky Hot Brown with Brown Beer Mornay

///

A Kentucky Hot Brown (sometimes known as a Hot Brown Sandwich) is a variation on the traditional Welsh rarebit. The Hot Brown was created at the Brown Hotel in Louisville, Kentucky, by Fred Schmidt in 1926. Inspired by the name, we chose brown ale for the mornay sauce.

The sandwich uses slices of a Pullman Loaf, which is bread baked in a lidded bread pan with straight sides. If you can't find a Pullman Loaf, substitute Texas toast.

Brown Beer Mornay Sauce

In a medium saucepan over medium heat, heat the milk until small bubbles form around the edge. In a second saucepan, melt the butter over low heat. Add the flour to the butter, mix well, and cook for 30 seconds on medium heat. Add the hot milk to the butter and flour and stir briskly until the mixture begins to thicken. Slowly whisk in the beer until it is fully incorporated. Add the shallot and nutmeg and cook on low for 20 minutes. Stir in the cheese and whisk until it is melted. Season to taste with salt and reserve for the sandwich.

Sandwich

Preheat the broiler. Toast the bread lightly. Top each slice of bread with half the sliced turkey. Cover each half with ¾ cup (6 fl oz/177 ml) of the Mornay Sauce. Broil the sandwiches until the mornay sauce begins to bubble and brown. Lay two slices each of the tomato and bacon over each sandwich. Finish with loads of freshly cracked black pepper.

ACTIVE PREP: 15 minutes
TOTAL TIME: 45 minutes + 16 hours
   for brining and chilling
SERVES: 2

IPA-BRINED VEGGIE RELISH

2 cup tomatoes, chopped
2 cup cabbage, chopped
1 cup onions, large diced
1 cup celery, large dice
1 cup cucumber, peeled and diced
½ cup green bell pepper, diced
¼ cup pickling salt
2 cup (16 fl oz/473 ml) red wine vinegar
2 cup (16 fl oz /473 ml) IPA
1 tsp celery seed
1 tsp mustard seed
1 tsp ground cinnamon
¼ tsp ground cloves
3 cloves garlic, crushed

SANDWICH

2 pieces focaccia 5" x 5" (13 cm x 13 cm)
2 oz (57 g) mortadella, sliced for sandwiches
2 oz (57 g) salami, sliced
3 oz (85 g) fresh mozzarella, sliced
2 oz (57 g) ham, sliced
2 oz (57 g) provolone, sliced
1 cup IPA-Brined Veggie Relish

Wicked Weed Pernicious IPA
(ASHEVILLE, NORTH CAROLINA)
Straight to Ale Monkeynaut IPA
(HUNTSVILLE, ALABAMA)

Muffaletta with IPA-Brined Veggie Relish

Muffaletta sandwiches can be found all over New Orleans, from delis and corner grocery stores to upscale restaurants. Here, we use more readily available focaccia for the bread, and we've replaced the traditional olive salad with an IPA-brined vegetable relish.

IPA-Brined Veggie Relish

In a large bowl, combine all the vegetables with the pickling salt and mix well. Allow to sit overnight.

In a large nonreactive pot, combine the remaining ingredients over medium heat and simmer for 10 minutes. Drain the vegetables from the night before, add them to the pot, and simmer for 30 minutes. Allow the relish to cool. Transfer the relish to a nonreactive container, cover, and chill overnight.

Sandwich

Cut each of the focaccia pieces in half horizontally. Layer the bottom half of the focaccia with the mortadella, salami, fresh mozzarella, ham, and provolone. Top with the relish and the top half of the focaccia.

Serve cold or warm up in a 300°F (149°C), although some hard-core muffaletta afficionados think it is blasphemy to heat the sandwich.

ACTIVE PREP: 20 minutes
TOTAL TIME: 35 minutes
SERVES: 4

SPICED LAMB PATTIES

1¾ lb (794 g) ground lamb
½ Tbs ground coriander
½ tsp ground cumin
¼ tsp ground cinnamon
1 tsp freshly ground black pepper
1 Tbs kosher salt
¼ cup (2 fl oz/59 ml) Belgian-style dubbel

RADISH SALAD

6 radishes, halved and sliced thin
1 shallot, julienned
1 lemon, zested and juiced
¼ cup picked parsley leaves
2 Tbs fresh mint, chopped
½ cup pistachios, toasted and chopped
¼ cup (2 fl oz/59 ml) olive oil
Kosher salt
Freshly ground black pepper

BURGERS

4 each 7 oz (198 g) Spiced Lamb Patties
4 Kaiser rolls, sesame seed rolls, or
  favorite burger bun, toasted
Pinch of salt
Freshly ground black pepper
4 Tbs Tahini paste

Westmalle Dubbel
(MALLE, BELGIUM)
The Lost Abbey Lost & Found
(SAN MARCOS, CALIFORNIA)
Achel Bruin
(HAMONT-ACHEL, BELGIUM)

Spiced Lamb Burgers with Tahini and Mint-Radish-Pistachio Salad

Spiced Lamb Patties

In a medium bowl, combine all the ingredients and mix well. Form into four 7-ounce (198 g) patties, about ¾ inch (19 mm) thick. Refrigerate while you prepare the Radish Salad.

Radish Salad

In a mixing bowl, combine the radish, shallot, lemon zest and juice, parsley, mint, pistachios, and olive oil and mix well. Season the radish salad with salt and freshly ground black pepper.

Burgers

Turn on the grill and heat on high. Grill the lamb patties to your desired doneness. Place each patty on a burger bun. Season to taste with salt and pepper. Top each patty with 1 tablespoon of tahini paste, then top each burger with the Radish Salad.

ACTIVE PREP: 15 minutes
TOTAL TIME: 45 minutes
SERVES: 4

1 lb (454 g) lobster meat (a mixture of tail, knuckle, and claw)
½ cup (4 fl oz/118 ml) mayonnaise
3 Tbs (1½ fl oz/44 ml) golden sour beer
½ cup celery, minced
2 Tbs parlsey, chopped
Pinch of cayenne
Dash of Worcestershire
Pinch of black pepper
2 Tbs butter, melted
4 hot dog buns, split top

New Belgium Brewing Le Terroir
(FORT COLLINS, COLORADO)
Lindemans Cuvée René
(VLEZENBEEK, BELGIUM)
Firestone Walker Agrestic
(PASO ROBLES, CALIFORNIA)

Sour Beer Lobster Rolls

A traditional lobster roll is a sandwich filled with butter-soaked lobster and served on a steamed (some say toasted) hot dog bun or similar roll. According to Food & Wine, *in Maine you're likely to find lobster rolls served one of two ways. Some "prefer a crunchy, tangy, and slightly spicy version of the lobster salad that includes celery, lettuce, lemon juice, and a pinch of cayenne. Purists leave out those ingredients because they believe nothing should interfere with the mix of sweet tender summer lobster and mayonnaise." Our recipe falls into the first camp, with sour beer and a pinch of cayenne to spice things up.*

Chop the large pieces of lobster meat into bite-size pieces. Combine the lobster with the mayonnaise, beer, celery, parsley, cayenne, Worcestershire, and black pepper. Mix well and chill for 30 minutes.

Brush the hot dog buns with the melted butter and toast. Top each bun with the chilled lobster salad.

ACTIVE PREP: 5 minutes
TOTAL TIME: 10 minutes
SERVES: 2

1 flatbread skin, about 12" x 5" (30 cm x 13 cm)
1–2 oz (28–57 g) goat cheese
1 side boneless smoked trout, crumbled
2 Tbs capers
2 Tbs red onion, sliced
2 Tbs basil chiffonade
Kosher salt
Freshly ground black pepper

Pair with:

New Belgium Abbey
(FORT COLLINS, COLORADO)
Allagash Dubbel
(PORTLAND, MAINE)
St. Bernardus 6
(WATOU, BELGIUM)

Smoked Trout Flatbread

Preheat the oven to 500°F (260°C). Using the back of a spoon, spread the goat cheese on the flatbread. Spread the crumbled trout, capers, and red onion liberally and evenly over the goat cheese.

Bake until the flatbread begins to brown. Remove from the oven, and sprinkle the basil evenly over the flatbread. Season to taste with salt and pepper.

ACTIVE PREP: 30 minutes
TOTAL TIME: 2 days
MAKES: 2 pint of relish, 8 large sandwiches

GIARDINIERA RELISH
2 cup small cauliflower florets
1 cup carrots, diced
1 cup celery, sliced on the bias
1 cup jarred pickled peperoncini, sliced + ½ cup (4 fl oz/118 ml) liquid
1 serrano pepper, sliced into thin rounds
1 cup green olives with pimento, sliced
2 cloves garlic, smashed
1½ cup (12 fl oz/355 ml) saison
½ tsp kosher salt
2 tsp dried oregano, divided
1 tsp celery salt
1 cup (8 fl oz/237 ml) extra virgin olive oil
1 Tbs (½ fl oz/15 ml) white wine vinegar

ITALIAN-STYLE BEEF SHORT RIBS
3 lb (1.4 kg) meaty boneless beef short ribs
2 tsp kosher salt, divided
Canola oil
1 yellow onion, sliced
3 carrots, sliced ¼" (6 mm) thick
2 stalks celery, sliced
½ tsp pepper
2 cloves garlic, minced
2 Tbs (1 fl oz/30 ml) tomato paste
One 15 oz (425 g) can crushed tomatoes
1 cup (8 fl oz/237 ml) beef broth
1 cup (8 fl oz/237 ml) barleywine
1 cup jarred roasted picquillo peppers, chopped + ½ cup (4 fl oz/118 ml) liquid
½ cup jarred peperoncini, sliced + ½ cup (4 fl oz/118 ml) liquid
2 bay leaves
2 sprigs fresh thyme
1 Tbs dried oregano
1 Tbs fresh parsley, minced
8 ciabatta rolls

Stone Brewing Co. Saison
(ESCONDIDO, CALIFORNIA)
Uinta Brewing Anniversary Barley Wine Ale
(SALT LAKE CITY, UTAH)

Italian-style Beef Short Ribs with Giardiniera Relish

Giardiniera Relish

Prepare all the vegetables. Place in a 1-gallon (3.8 l) sealable plastic bag. Combine the beer and pepper juice in a mixing bowl and stir in the kosher salt and 1 teaspoon oregano. The salt will make the mixture foam a bit. Pour the mixture into the bag with the vegetables, seal, and refrigerate overnight.

The next day, combine the remaining 1 teaspoon of oregano and celery salt with the olive oil and vinegar. Drain the beer brine from the vegetables. Discard the brine. Combine the brined vegetables with the oil mixture and place in an airtight container overnight. Giardiniera can be kept in an airtight container for up to two weeks.

Italian-style Beef Short Ribs

Preheat the oven to 325°F (163°C). Heat 2 tablespoons (1 fl oz/30 ml) canola oil in a Dutch oven over medium-high heat. Season the short ribs with 1 teaspoon of salt. Brown the short ribs in the canola oil, about 2 minutes per side. Cook in two batches if necessary to avoid overcrowding the pan. Remove the ribs to a bowl.

Reduce the heat slightly and add another tablespoon (½ fl oz/15 ml) of oil to the Dutch oven. Add the onion, carrot, and celery and cook 5 minutes until the vegetables start to get tender. Add 1 teaspoon salt and the ½ teaspoon pepper to the vegetables as they cook.

Add the garlic and cook 1–2 minutes until fragrant. Add the tomato paste and cook for 2 minutes stirring. Add the tomatoes, beef broth, barleywine, peppers, and pepper juices. Stir to combine and add the bay leaves, thyme, and dried oregano. Return to a boil. Place the meat back in the Dutch oven along with any accumulated juices and bring to a simmer. Remove from the heat and stir in the parsley. Cover and braise in the preheated oven for 2–2½ hours until meat is very tender.

Cool slightly, remove thyme sprigs and bay leaves. Shred the short ribs with two forks and return to the sauce. Serve on toasted ciabatta rolls with sauce and Giardiniera Relish.

ACTIVE PREP: 5 minutes
TOTAL TIME: 30 minutes
SERVES: 3-4

4 cup (32 fl oz/946 ml) water
4½ cup (36 fl oz/1 l) IPA
3 Tbs Old Bay Seasoning
1 lb (454 g) small Red Bliss potatoes
24 oz (680 g) smoked sausage, cut into 2"
  (5 cm) pieces
4 ears corn, halved
2 lb (907 g) shrimp, unpeeled
8 Tbs (1 stick) butter, softened
Kosher salt
Cocktail or horseradish sauce

Odell Rawah Rye IPA
(FORT COLLINS, COLORADO)
Founders Red Eye IPA
(GRAND RAPIDS, MICHIGAN)
Jester King Wytchmaker Farmhouse Rye IPA
(AUSTIN, TEXAS)

Frogmore Stew

Frogmore stew is named for a tiny town on the South Carolina coastal island of St. Helena. The one-pot dish, reputedly created in the 1950s by a local shrimp fisherman, calls for shrimp, corn on the cob, smoked sausage, and new potatoes steamed in a savory broth. Here IPA adds another layer of flavor.

In a large pot, combine the water, beer, and Old Bay and bring to a boil. Add the potatoes and boil for 10 minutes. Add the sausage and corn and continue boiling for 5 minutes. Add the shrimp and turn off the heat. Allow the stew to sit for 5 minutes.

Drain off all the liquid, add the butter, and stir to coat. Salt to taste. Pour the stew into a large serving bowl and serve with cocktail or horseradish sauce.

ACTIVE PREP: 20 minutes
TOTAL TIME: 40 minutes
SERVES: 6

4 Tbs butter
1 cup onion, diced
1 cup celery, diced
¼ cup flour
1½ cup (12 fl oz/355 ml) brown ale
2 cup (16 fl oz/473 ml) chicken stock
1 cup Idaho potato, diced
1 cup tomato, seeded and diced
3 oz (85 g) Swiss cheese, shredded
1 cup canned sauerkraut, drained
12 oz (340 g) corned beef, diced
1½ cup (12 fl oz/355 ml) heavy cream
Salt and pepper
Rye croutons

MadTree Gnarly Brown
(CINCINNATI, OHIO)
Epic Brewing Santa Cruz
(SALT LAKE CITY, UTAH)

Rueben Chowder

In a heavy-bottom pot, melt the butter over medium heat. Add the onion and celery and cook until the onions are soft, about 5 minutes. Add the flour and mix well.

Add the beer, chicken stock, potatoes, and tomatoes and reduce heat to simmer for 20 minutes. Add the Swiss cheese and stir until it melts into the soup. Add the sauerkraut, corned beef, and cream and bring to a simmer again for 5 minutes.

Season with salt and pepper. Serve in crocks and garnish with toasted rye croutons.

ACTIVE PREP: 60 minutes
TOTAL TIME: 8 hours
SERVES: 6–8

RED CHILE PURÉE
6 oz (170 g) dried New Mexico red chiles
Water

POSOLE
½ lb (227 g) pork butt, trimmed and cut into ½" (13 mm) cubes
2 Tbs (1 fl oz /30 ml) olive oil
2 large cloves garlic, minced
1 cup yellow onion, diced
6 oz (170 g) fresh tomatillos, papery skin removed, washed, and diced
3 Anaheim chiles, deseeded and diced
12 oz (340 g) posole/dried hominy, rinsed
4½ cup (36 fl oz/1 l) IPA
1 cup (8 fl oz/237 ml) Red Chile Purée
2 Tbs fresh oregano, chopped
Kosher salt
Shredded cabbage
Asadero cheese (an off-white, semi-firm Mexican cheese)
Tortillas

Ballast Point Habanero Sculpin IPA
(SAN DIEGO, CALIFORNIA)
Humboldt Nectar IPA
(PASO ROBLES, CALIFORNIA)

Beer and Pork Posole

Posole is a savory Mexican stew made from dried large white corn kernels also called posole or hominy. In our version, the red purée of dried New Mexico chiles gives the stew its kick, and the IPA adds a lightness and hops spiciness.

Red Chile Purée

Remove the stems and seeds from the red chiles. Place the chiles in a small pan with just enough water that the chiles start to float. Place the pan on high heat and boil for 30 minutes or until the chiles become tender. Remove from the heat and strain the chiles, making sure to reserve the liquid. Place the chiles in a blender and purée with just enough of the reserved liquid to create a smooth mixture. Reserve.

Posole

In a heavy bottom saucepan over medium-high heat, heat the oil and brown the pork. Add the garlic and onions and cook until translucent. Transfer the pork mixture to a slow cooker. Add the tomatillos, Anaheim chiles, posole, beer, and red chile purée.

With the lid on securely, cook on low (a slow simmer) for 7 hours. If you need to add a little liquid during the cooking process or at the end, add a little more beer. Add the oregano and season to taste with salt. Serve garnished with shredded cabbage and Asadero cheese and accompanied by warm tortillas.

ACTIVE PREP: 15 minutes
TOTAL TIME: 45 minutes
SERVES: 10–12

¼ lb (1 stick) butter
1 cup flour
¼ cup (2 fl oz/59 ml) olive oil
1 cup minced onion
½ cup minced celery
½ cup minced carrot
3 qt (96 fl oz/2.8 l) unsalted chicken
  stock/broth
2 cup (16 fl oz/473 ml) Belgian-style tripel
3 lb (1.4 kg) aged Gouda, shredded
Salt and white pepper
Toasted croutons or chopped bacon

Brouwerij Bosteels Tripel Karmeliet
(BUGGENHOUT, BELGIUM)
Allagash Tripel
(PORTLAND, MAINE)
New Belgium Trippel
(FORT COLLINS, COLORADO)

Aged Gouda & Beer Soup

//

In this variation of the pride of the Midwest, we combine aged Gouda with a Belgian-style tripel.

To make a blond roux with the butter and flour, in a medium saucepan over low heat, warm the butter gently until it melts. Whisk in the flour and cook for 1 minute. Remove from the heat and set aside.

In a heavy bottom saucepan over medium heat, sweat the onion, celery, and carrot in the olive oil until the onion is translucent. In a separate pan, bring the chicken stock to a boil and set aside.

Add the beer to the vegetables and bring to a boil. When the beer and vegetables have come to a boil, whisk in all the roux. Add the hot chicken stock to the beer and vegetable mixture and stir well, allowing the stock to thicken.

Simmer for 30 minutes over low heat. Slowly fold in the cheese and stir until all the cheese has melted. Season to taste with salt and white pepper.

Garnish with croutons or chopped bacon.

ACTIVE PREP: 15 minutes
TOTAL TIME: 2½–3 hours
SERVES: 6–8

4 lb (1.8 kg) yellow onions, julienned
4 Tbs (½ stick) butter
4 Tbs all-purpose flour
1½ cup (12 fl oz/355 ml) brown ale
1 oz (28 g) fresh Italian parsley
1 oz (28 g) fresh thyme
1 tsp black peppercorns
1 tsp whole mustard seed
4 whole allspice berries
2 cloves
2 qt (64 fl oz/1.9 l) beef stock
Croutons or sliced baguette
2 cup shredded Comté cheese

Humboldt Brown
(PASO ROBLES, CALIFORNIA)
Upslope Brown Ale
(BOULDER, COLORADO)

French Onion Soup with Brown Ale

///

There is nothing more comforting on a chilly autumn day than a bowl of hot French onion soup, especially one made with beer! Use a good beef stock (homemade is best) and take the time to caramelize the onions properly.

In a large pot over low heat, cook the onions in the butter, stirring occasionally. This process may take several hours to caramelize the onions properly.

Once onions have softened, reduced, and are the color of butterscotch, sift the flour evenly over the onions. Stir in the flour and let cook for 10 minutes. Stir in half the brown ale, scraping up any bits on the bottom of the pan. Increase the heat to medium, and bring to a simmer. Add the remaining brown ale and return to a simmer.

Create a sachet of the herbs and spices by wrapping them in cheesecloth and tying the bundle with twine. Add the sachet and the beef stock to the pot. Bring to a simmer and let cook for an hour.

Remove the sachet and serve the soup in crocks with croutons or sliced baguette and shredded Comté cheese.

ACTIVE PREP: 45 minutes
TOTAL TIME: 60 minutes
MAKES: 3 quart (96 fl oz/2.8 l)

CRAB SALAD

2 oz (57 g) crab meat, cooked
1 Tbs shallot, minced
4 cherry tomatoes, sliced in discs
1 Tbs fresh basil leaf, chopped
1 pinch cracked black pepper
1 pinch salt
Juice of half a lime
1 Tbs (½ fl oz/15 ml) olive oil

GRILLED CORN & BEER SOUP

12 ears fresh corn
½ cup (4 fl oz/118 ml) olive oil, divided
½ lb (227 g) smoked bacon, diced
2 cup onion, diced
1 jalapeño, roughly chopped
¼ cup garlic cloves, roughly chopped
4 cup (32 fl oz/946 ml) amber ale
4 cup (32 fl oz/946 ml) corn stock (see
   directions); you can also use chicken or
   vegetable stock
¼ cup (2 fl oz/59 ml) lime juice (about 2
   limes)
Salt

New Belgium Fat Tire Ale
(FORT COLLINS, COLORADO)
Alaskan Amber
(JUNEAU, ALASKA)
Odell 90 Shilling
(FORT COLLINS, COLORADO)

Spicy Grilled Corn & Beer Soup with Crab Salad

Crab Salad

Combine all the ingredients and mix well. Refrigerate until needed.

Grilled Corn & Beer Soup

Preheat the grill on high heat. Rub each ear of corn with a little olive oil and grill until the kernels begin to brown. Remove from the heat and allow to cool.

Holding the corn upright, with a sharp knife remove the kernels from the cob, keeping the knife as close to the cob as possible. This is where you'll get the natural cornstarch that will help thicken the soup without the need for a roux or cream. Place the cleaned cobs in a pot with 4 cups (32 fl oz/946 ml) of water and simmer for 30–45 minutes.

Preheat a large soup pot with ¼ cup (2 fl oz/59 ml) olive oil. Add the bacon and cook until the edges begin to brown. Add the onions and cook until translucent, being careful not to let them brown. Add the jalapeño and garlic and cook for 1 minute. Add the corn kernels, beer, and stock. Bring to a boil, then reduce to a simmer and cook for 30 minutes. Remove the soup from the heat. Working in batches, puree the soup in a blender until smooth. Strain through a metal sieve. Add the lime juice and season to taste with salt.

Ladle about a cup (8–10 fl oz/237–296 ml) of soup into each bowl and garnish each serving with the crab salad.

SUPPERS & DINNERS

ACTIVE PREP: 45 minutes
TOTAL TIME: 1 hour
SERVES: 4

1 shallot, sliced
1½ cup (12 fl oz/355 ml) blonde ale
1 cup (8 fl oz/237 ml) water
6 peppercorns
2 lemon slices
Four 6 oz (170 g) salmon fillets, skin off
Salt

HOPS BEARNAISE
1 small dried hops cone, crushed
¼ cup (2 fl oz/59 ml) white wine
1 shallot, halved
2 peppercorns
2 egg yolks
Juice of half a lemon
1½ cup (3 sticks) butter, melted
Tabasco
Salt

APPLE-FENNEL SLAW
1 green apple, thinly sliced
1 head of fennel, julienned
1 bunch arugula
2 Tbs (1 fl oz/30 ml) olive oil
1 Tbs (½ fl oz/15 ml) fresh lemon juice
Salt and fresh cracked black pepper

Ska Brewing True Blonde
(DURANGO, COLORADO)
Ommegang BPA or Fleur de Houblon
(COOPERSTOWN, NEW YORK)

Beer-Poached Salmon in Hops Bearnaise with Apple-Fennel Slaw

In a large pan, combine the shallot, ale, water, peppercorns, and lemon slices and heat on medium until bubbles begin to form on the bottom of the pan. Carefully add the salmon fillets to the poaching liquid and cook gently 8–10 minutes (there should be no bubbles or rolling water).

Gently remove the fish from the liquid with a perforated spatula and season lightly with salt.

Hops Bearnaise

In a small saucepan, combine the hops cone, wine, shallot, and peppercorns and reduce over medium heat until the pot is almost dry. Remove the shallot and peppercorns from the pot.

Combine the egg yolks and lemon juice in a stainless steel mixing bowl and whisk together.

In a pot, heat a cup (8 fl oz/237 ml) of water until it begins to steam. Place the mixing bowl on top of the steaming pot and whisk the egg yolks until the eggs begin to resemble ribbons. Remove from the heat and slowly whisk in the butter, 1 tablespoon at a time. Once the butter is incorporated, add the remains of the pot with the wine and hops and a dash of Tabasco. Season with salt.

Apple-Fennel Slaw

In a small mixing bowl, combine the apple, fennel, arugula, olive oil, and lemon juice and mix well. Season with salt and pepper.

To serve, place one salmon fillet on each plate. Top with 4–6 tablespoons (2–3 fl oz/59–89 ml) Bernaise sauce. Add Apple-Fennel Slaw alongside.

ACTIVE PREP: 35 minutes
TOTAL TIME: 50 minutes
SERVES: 1–2

4–5 U/20 scallops
10 Brussels sprouts, ends cut off and
   blanched in salted water until tender

SMOKY MUSSEL MÄRZEN BROTH

1 small onion, sliced
2 cloves garlic, smashed and chopped
½ lb (227 g) mussels
2 Tbs butter, divided
1½ cup (12 fl oz/355 ml) Märzen beer
1 Tbs (½ fl oz/15 ml) Dijon mustard
½ tsp red chili flakes
½ tsp fennel seed
1 Tbs (½ fl oz/15 ml) honey
1 sprig tarragon
Small handful of applewood chips soaked
   in water, then drained
Canola or grapeseed oil

Brouwerij Bosteels Tripel Karmeliet
(BUGGENHOUT, BELGIUM)
Victory Golden Monkey
(DOWNINGTOWN, PENNSYLVANIA)
Allagash Tripel
(PORTLAND, MAINE)

Scallops and Brussels in a Smoky Mussel Märzen Broth

In a medium pan, heat 1 tablespoon of butter over medium heat. Sauté the onions, garlic, and mussels. Add the beer, mustard, chili flakes, fennel seed, honey, and tarragon. Steam until the mussels just begin to open.

Remove the mussels from the broth and pull the meat out of the mussels (save the shells) and set the mussels aside in a little of the broth.

In a stove-top smoker, smoke the mussel shells over the applewood chips for 10 minutes. Add the smoked shells to the broth and simmer for another 10 minutes.

Strain the broth from the shells and add the mussel meat to the smoky broth. Set aside.

Coat the bottom of a small sauté pan with canola or grapeseed oil and heat over medium-high heat until the oil shimmers. Sauté the scallops on one side to caramelize. Remove from the pan. Sauté the Brussels in the same pan, then add the mussels, broth, and scallops to the pan. Finish with the remaining tablespoon of butter.

ACTIVE PREP: 20 minutes
TOTAL TIME: 30 minutes
SERVES: 2

WHEAT-BEER BROTH

1 shallot, chopped
2–3 cloves garlic, chopped
2 tsp canola oil
2 sprigs thyme
1 Tbs (½ fl oz/15 ml) honey
2 Tbs (1 fl oz/30 ml) Dijon mustard
1 tsp chili flakes
1½ cup (12 fl oz/355 ml) wheat beer
1 cup (8 fl oz/237 ml) bottled clam juice

COMPLETE DISH

2 Tbs (1 fl oz/30 ml) grapeseed oil
1 lb (454 g) fresh mussels, black, blue, or
  green-lipped, East or West Coast
1 bunch kale, roughly chopped
Two 4" (10 cm) hot smoked sausage links,
  cut into ¼" (6 mm) bias slices

Bell's Oberon Ale
(KALAMAZOO, MICHIGAN)
Modern Times Fortunate Islands
(SAN DIEGO, CALIFORNIA)

Mussels, Hot Smoky Links, and Kale with Dijon Wheat-Beer Broth

Wheat-Beer Broth

Heat a pan over medium-low heat until hot. Add the oil to the pan and swirl to coat. Add the shallot and garlic and sweat until they start to caramelize. Add the remaining ingredients and simmer for 10 minutes.

Complete Dish

In a large pan, heat the grapeseed oil over high heat. Sauté the mussels, kale, and sausages until the mussels begin to open. Deglaze with the Wheat-Beer Broth and serve with crusty bread.

ACTIVE PREP: 25 minutes
TOTAL TIME: 35 minutes
SERVES: 2

2 Tbs (1 fl oz/30 ml) olive oil
Two 4 oz (113 g) pieces of fresh cod or
  other white fish
Kosher salt
6 oz (170 g) bulk chorizo sausage
1 Tbs garlic, minced
½ lb (227 g) black mussels, rinsed clean
2 Roma tomatoes, diced
2 Tbs parsley, chopped
1½ cup (12 fl oz/355 ml) saison
Juice of half a lemon
6 Tbs butter, chilled
6 oz (170 g) cooked fettuccini

Boulevard Tank 7
(KANSAS CITY, MISSOURI)
Funkwerks Saison
(FORT COLLINS, COLORADO)
Firestone Walker Opal
(PASO ROBLES, CALIFORNIA)
Saison Dupont
(TOURPES, BELGIUM)

Seared Cod with Mussels, Chorizo, Noodles, and Beer Butter Sauce

Place the olive oil into a medium sauté pan and heat on high. Season the cod with a pinch of salt. Once you begin to see wisps of smoke in the pan, place the cod, gently and carefully, in the pan. Do not shake the pan. Allow the fish to caramelize and pull off the pan organically, 2–3 minutes. Turn the fish over and repeat the process on the second side until it is cooked through. Remove the fish to a paper towel to rest while you finish the dish.

Lower the heat to medium high, add the chorizo to the pan and cook through, breaking it up into small pieces. Add the garlic, mussels, tomatoes, and a pinch of salt and cook for 1 minute. Add the parsley and beer and reduce the heat to low.

Reduce the liquid by half. Stir in the lemon juice. Remove the pan from the heat and whisk in the butter until it has melted completely and thickened the sauce. Add a pinch of salt. Add the fettuccini and toss together until the fettuccini is coated. Divide the contents of the pan evenly onto two plates. Top with the seared cod and serve.

ACTIVE PREP: 40 minutes
TOTAL TIME: 45 minutes
SERVES: 3–4

SEASONED FLOUR
3 cup all-purpose flour
2 Tbs onion powder
2 Tbs garlic powder
2 tsp paprika
2 tsp salt
2 tsp white pepper

BEER BATTER
3 1/3 cup all-purpose flour
¾ cup rice flour
2 tsp baking powder
4 cup (32 fl oz/946 ml) American lager
½ cup (4 fl oz/118 ml) vodka
1 Tbs (½ fl oz/15 ml) honey

FISH FRY
1 lb (454 g) cod or haddock fillets, cut
　into about 3 oz (85 g) portions
Seasoned flour
Beer batter
Canola oil to fill a deep fat fryer

New Glarus Two Women
(NEW GLARUS, WISCONSIN)
August Schell Pilsner
(NEW ULM, MINNESOTA)
Guinness Blonde
(DUBLIN, IRELAND)

Wisconsin Beer-Battered Fish Fry

Adding beer to fish batter enhances the texture of the fried fish because when the fish hits the hot oil, carbon dioxide in the beer is released, creating air in the coating. This then provides a nice light crunch without overcooking the fish.

Seasoned Flour
Mix all the ingredients in a bowl with a dry whisk and reserve.

Beer Batter
In a bowl, whisk together the flours and baking powder. In a separate bowl, whisk together the beer, vodka, and honey. Slowly whisk the dry ingredients into the wet ingredients to make a batter.

Fish Fry
Fill the fryer with oil and heat to 350°F (177°C) following the manufacturer's directions. Arrange the bowls of fish, seasoned flour, and batter with the fish farthest from the fryer, then the seasoned flour, and then the beer batter. With tongs or fingers, take one piece of fish at a time, dip the fish into the seasoned flour to coat, then into the beer batter, and then slowly drop the fish into the hot oil, avoiding splashes. Fry the fish for 3–4 minutes until cooked all the way through. Carefully remove the fish and drain on paper towels. Repeat with each piece of fish.

ACTIVE PREP: 15 minutes
TOTAL TIME: 25 minutes
SERVES: 1–2

CAST IRON RIB-EYE

2 Tbs butter
One 12 oz (340 g) boneless rib-eye (14 oz/397 g bone in)
¼ cup (2 fl oz/59 ml) IPA
1 pinch salt
1 pinch freshly ground black pepper
¼ cup (2 fl oz/59 ml) Blue Cheese–Beer Butter (see below)

BLUE CHEESE-BEER BUTTER

½ lb butter (2 sticks), room temperature
¼ lb (113 g) blue cheese crumbles
¼ cup (2 fl oz/59 ml) IPA
1 tsp kosher salt
2 Tbs parsley, chopped

Cook with:
Victory DirtWolf
(DOWNINGTOWN, PENNSYLANIA)
Lagunitas Sucks
(PETALUMA, CALIFORNIA)
Schlafly Tasmanian IPA
(ST. LOUIS, MISSOURI)

Pair with:
Firestone Walker Wookey Jack
(PASO ROBLES, CALIFORNIA)
Odell Brewing Mountain Standard
(FORT COLLINS, COLORADO)

Cast Iron Rib-Eye with Blue Cheese–Beer Butter

Place the butter in a large cast-iron pan and place the pan over high heat. Once the pan begins to smoke, gently lay the rib-eye in the pan and brown the bottom. Turn the steak over and cook to desired doneness, being careful to avoid splattering the hot butter.

Remove from the heat just before the rib-eye reaches your desired internal temperature (130–135°F/55–57°C for medium-rare; 160°F/71°C for well-done). Deglaze the pan with the beer, then season the steak with the salt and pepper. Place the Blue Cheese–Beer Butter on the steak and allow it to melt slowly while serving.

Blue Cheese–Beer Butter

Combine all the ingredients in a tabletop mixer or food processor and blend together. Remove and chill until the butter sets.

ACTIVE PREP: 45 minutes

TOTAL TIME: 36–38 hours (including brining and roasting the brisket)

SERVES: 10–12

PORTER BRINE

1 gal (128 fl oz/3.8 l) water

¾ cup salt

½ cup sugar

3 tsp pink curing salt

1 yellow onion

6–8 cloves garlic

1 Tbs coriander

1 Tbs chicory coffee

4 bay leaves

1 Tbs black pepper

2 qt (64 fl oz/1.9 l) porter

2 qt (64 fl oz/1.9 l) ice

1 beef brisket (8–10 lb/3.6–4.5 kg), trimmed

CINNAMON TRUFFLE SQUASH PUREE

2 acorn squash

1 Tbs butter

¼ tsp ground cinnamon

¼ tsp white truffle oil

Salt and pepper to taste

½ cup (4 fl oz/118 ml) heavy cream

Anchor Porter

(SAN FRANCISCO, CALIFORNIA)

Deschutes Black Butte Porter

(BEND, OREGON)

Founders Porter

(GRAND RAPIDS, MICHIGAN)

Porter-Brined Brisket with Cinnamon Truffle Squash Puree

///

Porter Brine

Combine the water, sugar, and salt in a nonreactive pot. Bring to a boil and stir to dissolve the sugar and salt. Remove from the heat and add the remaining ingredients except the beer, ice, and brisket. Let steep for 30 minutes. Stir in the beer and ice and cool the brine to 45°F (7°C) or lower.

Add the brisket and brine refrigerated for 24 hours. Strain off the brine and reserve half to reduce for the sauce.

Mark the brisket on the grill, then cover it with parchment and foil and roast with the fat cap side up at 240°F (116°C) for 10–12 hours.

Remove from the oven. Let the brisket rest and cool completely. Bring the reserved brine to a boil, reduce heat and simmer until reduced by half. Mix the reduction with juices from the roast. Slice the brisket and serve.

Cinnamon Truffle Squash Puree

Cut each squash in half and scoop out the seeds. Butter the inside of the squash and roast at 400°F (204°C) for about 30 minutes. Remove from the oven and let the squash cool slightly. Scoop out the flesh and discard the skin. Puree the squash in a food processor with the remaining ingredients until smooth.

Spoon squash puree into a serving bowl and serve alongside the brisket.

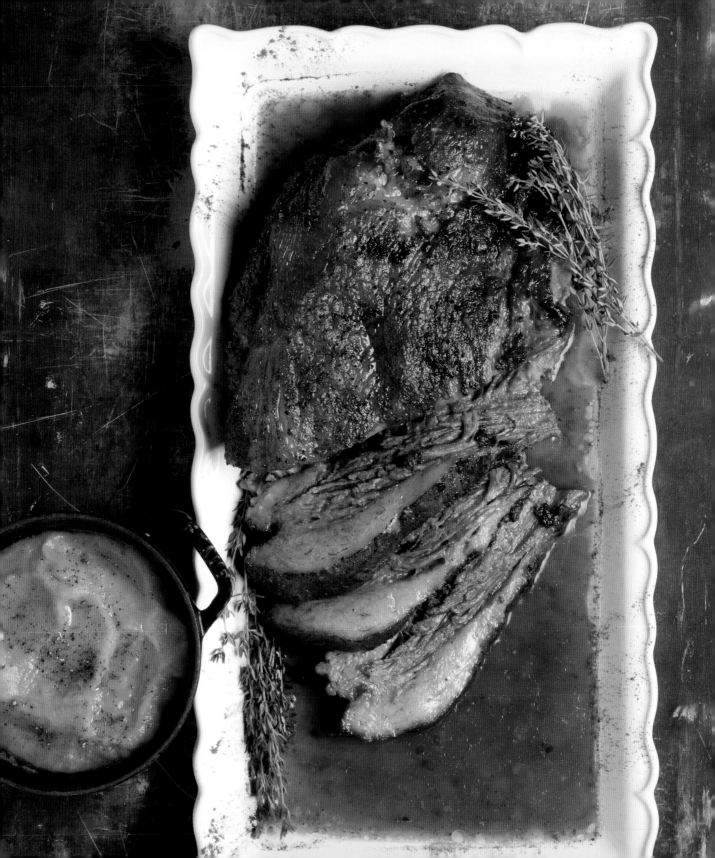

ACTIVE PREP: 35 minutes
TOTAL TIME: 3½ hours
SERVES: 4

½ cup (4 fl oz/118 ml) olive oil
2 lb (907 g) beef short ribs, boneless
1 cup all-purpose flour
1 yellow onion, large dice
1 large carrot, large dice
2 celery stalks, large dice
1 lb (454 g) Yukon gold potatoes, halved
½ lb (227 g) white mushrooms, quartered
2 oz (57 g) pearl onions (frozen is okay)
4 cup (32 fl oz/946 ml) Märzen beer
2 sprigs rosemary
1 sheet puff pastry dough
1 egg, whipped
Salt

Surly Brewing Surlyfest
(MINNEAPOLIS, MINNESOTA)
Great Lakes Oktoberfest
(CLEVELAND, OHIO)
Neshaminy Creek Creekfestbier
(CROYDON, PENNSYLVANIA)

Short Rib Pot Pie

Preheat oven to 325°F (163°C).

Heat the olive oil in a large pan over medium-high heat. Dredge the short ribs in the flour and brown in the hot pan. Once browned, place the short ribs in a large baking dish.

Add the onions, carrots, celery, potatoes, mushrooms, and pearl onions to the hot pan. Cook until they begin to brown. Deglaze the pan with 1 cup (8 fl oz/237 ml) of beer.

Pour the vegetables into the baking dish on top of the short ribs. Add the remaining beer and the rosemary. Cover and place in the preheated oven. Cook for 2½ hours.

Remove the dish from the oven. Carefully pull the short ribs out of the dish and shred either by hand or with a knife. Return the ribs to the dish and mix well. Season with salt.

From the puff pastry dough, cut a top the size of the baking dish. Top the dish with the pastry dough, brush with the egg, and return to oven. Bake for 20 minutes or until the pastry becomes brown. (If you prefer, you can bake the puff pastry separately and top once the shortribs have cooked for 3 hours.)

ACTIVE PREP: 25 minutes
TOTAL TIME: 2–4 hours
SERVES: 4–6

1 small bunch fresh thyme, about 1 oz (28 g)
1 cup kosher salt
½ cup white sugar
1 sirloin roast, 3–4 lb (1.4–1.8 kg)
1½ cup (12 fl oz/355 ml) imperial stout
1 yellow onion, diced
3 celery stalks, sliced ½" (13 mm) thick

Epic Brewing Big Bad Baptist
(SALT LAKE CITY, UTAH)
Goose Island Bourbon Co. Coffee Stout
(CHICAGO, ILLINOIS)
Founders KBS
(GRAND RAPIDS, MICHIGAN)

Stout Roast Beef

Coarsely chop the fresh thyme and mix it with the salt and sugar. Rub the mixture liberally over the roast and let it sit at room temperature for at least 1 hour and up to 3 hours. Then scrape most of the mixture off of the roast, but do not rinse.

Preheat the oven to 350°F (177°C). Over medium-high heat in a sauté pan large enough to hold the roast, sear the roast on all sides. In a baking pan large enough to hold the roast, arrange the roast, beer, onion, and celery. Cover with foil.

Bake until the internal temperature reaches 135°F (57°C) for medium rare (50–80 minutes). Remove the pan from the oven and transfer the roast to a platter. Cover the roast with foil and let it rest for 10–15 minutes. Reserve the cooking juices. Slice the roast and serve it and the reserved cooking juices with Charred Broccoli and Beer-Barley Salad (page 62).

ACTIVE PREP: 15 minutes
TOTAL TIME: 50 minutes
SERVES: 2

2 boneless chicken breasts, skin on
Salt and pepper to taste
1 Tbs flour
1 Tbs (½ fl oz/15 ml) oil
1 small onion, ¼" (6 mm) dice
2 cloves garlic, minced
2 tsp fresh ginger, grated
12–15 dried apricots, sliced
1 tsp Dijon mustard
½ cup (4 fl oz/118 ml) chicken stock
½ cup (4 fl oz/118 ml) IPA
2 Tbs (1 fl oz/30 ml) heavy cream
1 Tbs unsalted butter
Salt and pepper to taste

Dogfish Head ApriHop
(MILTON, DELAWARE)
Bell's Two Hearted Ale
(KALAMAZOO, MICHIGAN)

Crispy Chicken with Apricot IPA Sauce

Preheat the oven to 375°F (190°C).

Season both sides of the chicken breasts with salt and pepper. Lightly dredge the chicken breasts in flour and shake off any excess. In a heavy ovenproof skillet, heat the oil over medium-high heat.

Using tongs, add the chicken breasts to the pan, skin side down. Move the chicken breasts slightly in the pan to ensure that they are not sticking. Brown the chicken breasts and render fat, about 6–8 minutes. Turn the chicken breasts and cook on the second side until evenly browned, about 4 minutes.

Transfer the pan to the preheated oven for 12–15 minutes to finish cooking. The internal temperature should read at least 160°F (71°C) on an instant-read thermometer inserted into the thickest part of the breast.

Remove the chicken breasts to a plate and tent with foil to keep warm. Place the skillet on a burner set to medium heat. Add the onion and cook 1–2 minutes. Add the garlic and ginger and cook until fragrant, 1–2 minutes. Add the chicken stock and IPA to the skillet to deglaze the pan. Stir in the Dijon mustard and apricots and season with salt and pepper. Bring the sauce to a simmer and reduce by half. Add the heavy cream and butter and stir to incorporate and warm. Remove the pan from the heat.

Spoon some sauce onto center of a plate. Place a chicken breast on the sauce, skin side up. Add more sauce around the chicken breast and serve.

ACTIVE PREP: 20 minutes
TOTAL TIME: About 5 days (including fermenting the chilies)
SERVES: 6–8

HITACHINO SWEET SAUCE

1 lb (454 g) Fresno chilies, cut in half lengthwise and seeded

2 Tbs kosher salt

¼ tsp xanthum gum powder

¼ tsp citric acid

1½ cup (12 fl oz/355 ml) Hitachino Nest White Ale (or other witbier)

1 cup (8 fl oz/237 ml) agave syrup

1 Tbs garlic, chopped

MICHELADA BRINE

1 qt (32 fl oz/946 ml) water

6 cup (48 fl oz/1.4 l) light lager

Juice of 6 limes

½ cup salt

¼ cup granulated sugar

Two 3–4 lb (1.4–1.8 kg) chickens, whole

For the brine:
Ska Brewing Mexican Logger
(DURANGO, COLORADO)

Pair with an India pale lager:
Jack's Abby Hoponius Union
(FRAMINGHAM, MASSACHUSETTS)
Founders Dissenter
(GRAND RAPIDS, MICHIGAN)

Michelada Chicken with Hitachino Sweet Sauce

The michelada, one of the most popular drinks in Mexico, is a beer-based cocktail. Its recipe usually includes lime juice and chilies. In our riff on this base, we marinate the chicken in beer and lime juice, then serve it with a sweet beer-chili sauce.

Hitachino Sweet Sauce

Before all of this begins, a great start for extra flavor will be fermenting chilies for the sweet beer sauce, which can take 3–5 days depending on the climate where you live and your kitchen temperature.

Place the chilies in a nonreactive container, sprinkle with the salt, and toss together. Fill a gallon (3.8 l) zipper-lock bag half full with water and place it on top of the chilies to weigh them down. Let sit at room temperature for 3–5 days.

Skim any muck from the top of the chilies, then cook the chilies in their liquid for 10 minutes until soft. This strips most of the good fermentation *Lactobacillus,* but it ensures that the sauce is safe (for the quasi-squeamish). Set the chilies aside until the chickens are roasted.

While the roasted chickens rest, puree the chilies in a food processor with the xanthum gum powder, citric acid, beer, agave syrup, garlic, and the drippings from the roast chickens. Taste and adjust seasoning with salt if necessary.

Michelada Brine

In a nonreactive bowl, combine all the ingredients except the chickens and mix well. Add the chickens, turning to coat. Refrigerate and brine for at least 4 hours.

Roast the chickens at 400°F (204°C) until juices run clear from the leg (60–80 minutes). Transfer the chickens to a platter and cover with foil while you finish the Hitachino Sweet Sauce using the drippings.

To serve, arrange the chickens on a serving platter and pour the Hitachino Sweet Sauce over. Garnish with arugula, baby mustard greens, or grilled dandelion greens.

ACTIVE PREP: 40 minutes
TOTAL TIME: 1½ hours
SERVES: 4–6

MOLASSES PORTER QUAIL

½ cup (4 fl oz/118 ml) porter

½ cup (4 fl oz/118 ml) molasses

4 semi-boneless quail, halved, backbone and breastplate removed

1 lb (454 g) mixed greens

¾ cup (6 fl oz/177 ml) Maibock Vinaigrette (see below)

1 red bell pepper, minced

Kosher salt

Fresh cracked black pepper

MAIBOCK VINAIGRETTE

2 small shallots, chopped

2 cloves garlic

¼ cup (2 fl oz/59 ml) Maibock

½ cup (4 fl oz/118 ml) balsamic vinegar

½ cup (4 fl oz/118 ml) olive oil

¼ cup (2 fl oz/59 ml) canola oil

Kosher salt

Black pepper

Sierra Nevada Porter
(CHICO, CALIFORNIA)
Fort Collins Brewery Maibock
(FORT COLLINS, COLORADO)

Pair with:
Southern Tier Live
(LAKEWOOD, NEW YORK)
Sweetwater 420
(ATLANTA, GEORGIA)

Molasses Porter Quail with Baby Lettuces and Maibock Vinaigrette

Molasses Porter Quail

Combine the porter and molasses and mix well. Add the quail to the porter mixture and let marinate for 1 hour. While the quail marinate, make the Maibock Vinaigrette.

Remove the quail from the marinade, reserving the marinade. Turn the grill to high. Grill the quail until done, brushing with the marinade as you go.

Toss the greens with the Maibock Vinaigrette and red pepper and arrange on a platter. Sprinkle with salt and fresh cracked black pepper. Lay the quail over the greens and serve.

Maibock Vinaigrette

In a blender, combine the shallots, garlic, Maibock, and vinegar. Puree until smooth. Mix the olive oil and canola oil in a small bowl. With the blender on low speed, slowly drizzle the oil into the blender until fully incorporated and emulsified. Season with salt and pepper.

ACTIVE PREP: 15 minutes
TOTAL TIME: 8 hours
SERVES: 4

RIB RUB

1 Tbs chili powder
2 tsp garlic powder
1 tsp ground mustard
1 tsp ground cumin
1 tsp salt
½ tsp pepper
1/8 tsp cayenne pepper
1 Tbs brown sugar

RIBS & SAUCE

1 full rack baby back ribs (about 4 lb/1.8
  kg), silver skin removed
1½ cup (12 fl oz/355 ml) porter
Barbeque sauce

Deschutes Brewery Black Butte Porter
(BEND, OREGON)
Odell Brewing Company 90 Shilling
(FORT COLLINS, COLORADO)
Kona Brewing Company Pipeline Porter
(KAILUA-KONA, HAWAII)

Porter Braised and Grilled Baby Back Ribs

Combine the rub ingredients in a small bowl. Rub the ribs thoroughly with the mixture (you may not need all the rub for this recipe). Wrap the ribs in plastic and place them in the refrigerator for at least 6 hours and up to one day.

Preheat the oven to 375°F (190°C). Remove the ribs from the plastic and place them in a roasting pan, bone-side down.

In a small saucepan over medium-high heat, bring the porter to a simmer being careful not to let it boil over. Pour the beer around the ribs. Seal the roasting pan tightly with foil. Braise the ribs in the beer for 1 hour and 45 minutes, or until tender. Remove the ribs to a platter and pour the beer and accumulated pan juices into a saucepan. Simmer over low heat to reduce the sauce. Add ¼ cup (2 fl oz/59 ml) of your favorite barbeque sauce to the mixture and stir to combine.

Heat your grill or broiler to medium-high. Brush the ribs with the reduced sauce and grill or broil the ribs until the sauce is brown and bubbly, about 3 minutes per side. Remove the ribs from the grill or broiler and brush them with additional sauce. Cut into individual ribs and serve.

ACTIVE PREP: 25 minutes
TOTAL TIME: 3 hours
SERVES: 8–10

One 8–10 lb (3.6–4.5 kg) boneless ham,
  fully cooked
3 cup (24 fl oz/710 ml) hard cider
½ cup dark brown sugar
¾ cup (6 fl oz/177 ml) orange juice
½ cup (4 fl oz/118 ml) apple jelly, warmed
1 tsp allspice, ground
3 cloves, whole

Cook with:
Angry Orchard Stone Dry
(WALDEN, NEW YORK)

Pair with:
Deschutes Abyss
(BEND, OREGON)
New Belgium La Folie
(FORT COLLINS, COLORADO)

Hard-Cider Glazed Ham

Preheat the oven to 325°F (163°C). Score the ham, being careful not to cut into the meat. Place the ham in a roasting pan with 1 cup (8 fl oz/237 ml) of the hard cider. Bake for 2 hours or to an internal temperature of 145°F (63°C).

While the ham is baking, combine the remaining cider, sugar, orange juice, apple jelly, allspice, and cloves in a small saucepan. Bring to a boil, then reduce to a simmer for 10 minutes. When the ham reaches the designated temperature, use a pastry brush to brush the ham with the glaze. Reduce the oven heat to 250°F (121°C) and bake for an additional 30 minutes, glazing the ham every 5–7 minutes.

Remove from oven, slice and serve.

ACTIVE PREP: 55 minutes
TOTAL TIME: 27 hours
MAKES: 10–12 sausages

5 lb (2.3 kg) pork butt
1½ cup (12 fl oz/355 ml) stout
¼ cup garlic, minced
1 tsp freshly ground black pepper
1 tsp cayenne pepper
¼ tsp dried thyme
1 Tbs paprika
¼ tsp crushed bay leaf
¼ tsp dried sage
2 Tbs salt
1½ yd (91 cm) pork casing

High Hops Brewing The Dark One
(WINDSOR, COLORADO)
Mad River Steelhead Extra Stout
(BLUE LAKE, CALIFORNIA)
Tallgrass Brewing Buffalo Sweat
(MANHATTAN, KANSAS)

Stout-Brined Andouille Sausage

//

French in origin, Andouille sausage has become closely associated with Louisiana Creole cuisine. Instead of smoking, we brine the pork in stout before stuffing the casings and then grill the sausages.

Cut the pork butt into about 2" × 2" (5 cm × 5 cm) pieces and place in a mixing bowl. Add the beer, garlic, herbs, spices, and salt and mix well. Refrigerate for 12 hours then move the seasoned pork to the freezer for 2 hours.

Remove the sausage mixture from the freezer and pass it through a food grinder fitted with a fine blade. Using a hand stuffer, fill the pork casing with the pork mixture. Twist and tie off to make 4–6-inch (10–15 cm) sausages. Store uncovered in the refrigerator for 12 hours.

Heat the grill to high. Grill the sausages until they are cooked through.

ACTIVE PREP: 35 minutes
TOTAL TIME: 6½ hours
SERVES: 4–6

5 lb (2.3 kg) bone-in pork ribs, cut about 1"
(2.5 cm) thick

RUB
4 Tbs sea salt
3 Tbs brown sugar
1 Tbs black Tellicherry pepper

BEER CARAMEL
1 cup sugar
1½ cup (12 fl oz/355 ml) pale lager beer
1 Tbs butter
½ cup (4 fl oz/118 ml) heavy cream
1 Tbs salt
1 Tbs garlic, minced
1 Tbs fresh ginger, grated
1 tsp sambal (a spicy Southeast Asian
   condiment that you can find at your
   local Asian market)

WINTER MELON PICKLE
6 cup (48 fl oz/1.4 l) water
2 cup (16 fl oz/473 ml) vinegar
2 Tbs salt
2 cup sugar
1 Tbs toasted coriander seed
2 lemon rinds
1 winter melon, peeled and diced
¼ cup fresh mint leaves, torn

Victory Lager
(DOWNINGTOWN, PENNSYLANIA)
The Bruery Humulous Lager
(PLACENTIA, CALIFORNIA)

Pork Ribs with Beer Caramel and Winter Melon Pickle

Rub
Season the ribs and grill them long enough to mark them. Place the ribs in a roasting pan, cover with parchment and foil, and roast in a 240°F (115°C) oven for about 6 hours.

Beer Caramel
Caramelize the sugar in a heavy-bottom pan over low heat until it is golden and smooth. Add the beer, butter, cream, salt, garlic, ginger, and sambal. Simmer and stir until combined evenly.

Winter Melon Pickle
Winter melons are, as their name implies, cold season melons. They have a hard, thin, green skin with a waxy feel. Their white flesh is mild flavored with a similar water-rich texture of a watermelon. Find them at your local Asian market or in the specialty produce section of your grocery store.

Combine all the ingredients except the winter melon and mint leaves in a nonreactive saucepan and simmer for 10 minutes. Cool and stir in the winter melon and mint leaves. Refrigerate for 2 hours.

Place 4–5 ribs on each plate, top with Beer Caramel and Winter Melon Pickle, and garnish with sliced red onion.

ACTIVE PREP: 20 minutes
TOTAL TIME: 12–14 hours
SERVES: 4

BEER AND BACON PINTO BEANS
2 cup pinto beans
3 cup (24 fl oz/710 ml) wheat beer
Smoked bacon, thick cut
Salt and pepper
Ketchup for serving

CORNBREAD
2¼ cup all-purpose flour
⅔ cup cornmeal
1½ tsp baking powder
1 tsp salt
½ cup sugar
5 eggs
2 cup (16 fl oz/473 ml) milk
¾ cup (6 fl oz/177 ml) grapeseed oil

Aecht Schlenkerla Rauchbier Weizen
(BAMBERG, BAVARIA)
Schneider Weiss Tap 6 Aventinus
(KELHEIM, GERMANY)

Beer and Bacon Pinto Beans with Cornbread

///

Beer and Bacon Pinto Beans

Place the beans in a soup pot. Fill the pot with water to cover the beans with at least 2 inches (5 cm) of water. Soak for 8–12 hours. Drain and rinse the beans, then return them to the pot, add the beer and bacon and more water to cover the beans. Simmer for about 2 hours or until tender. Season with salt and pepper.

Cornbread

Assemble the cornbread batter a few minutes before the beans are fully cooked and tender.

In a medium bowl, combine the flour, cornmeal, baking powder, salt, and sugar. Mix well. In another bowl, combine the eggs, milk, and grapeseed oil. Add the wet ingredients to the dry ingredients and stir until well combined.

When the beans are fully cooked and tender, pour them into a cast-iron skillet and top with the cornbread batter. Bake at 375°F (191°C) for about 20 minutes, until golden brown.

Serve with ketchup. It's simple but very delicious.

ACTIVE PREP: 50 minutes
TOTAL TIME: 2 hours
SERVES: 3–4

2 Idaho potatoes, scrubbed
2 egg yolks, lightly beaten
1 cup 00 (extra-fine) flour
1 tsp salt
½ tsp black pepper
1 cup grated Parmesan cheese
Olive oil
6 cup (48 fl oz/1.4 l) pilsner
Oil for frying
4 Tbs (½ stick) butter
Salt and pepper to taste
1 lemon
4 Tbs (2 fl oz/59 ml) sour cream
4 Tbs minced chives

Cook with:
New Belgium Blue Paddle
(FORT COLLINS, COLORADO)

Pair with:
Ayinger Celebrator
(AYING, GERMANY)
Epic Double Skull
(SALT LAKE CITY, UTAH)

Beer-Cheese Gnocchi in Crispy Potato Skins

In Italy, flour is classified by how finely ground it is and how much of the bran and wheat germ have been removed. Doppio zero (00) flour is the most highly refined and is powder soft. If you can't find it, substitute all-purpose flour.

Roast the potatoes at 350°F (177°C) for 1 hour. Transfer to a wire rack and let them cool until they are still hot but cool enough to handle. Cut the potatoes in half and scoop out the flesh, leaving ⅛–¼ inch (3–6 mm) intact to make potato skins. Set aside the potato skins.

In a small bowl, mash the potatoes with a fork and add the egg yolks, flour, salt, pepper, Parmesan cheese, and 1 teaspoon olive oil. Fold everything together to make a warm potato dough. Don't overwork the dough; just bring all the ingredients together.

Flour your work surface and roll the dough out to about ½-inch (13 mm) thickness. Cut the dough into ½-inch (13 mm) strips and roll the strips slightly to form ropes. Cut the ropes into ½-inch (13 mm) pieces.

In a nonreactive pot, heat 5¼ cup (42 fl oz/1.2 l) of beer to a simmer. Add the gnocchi pieces to the simmering beer and cook until they float. Scoop out the gnocchi with a slotted spoon, toss them with olive oil, and spread them out on a cookie sheet to cool.

In a deep fryer or skillet filled with oil, fry the potato skins until crispy. Drain and cool slightly.

Sauté the blanched gnocchi in 1 tablespoon of butter until they start to brown; season with salt and pepper. Divide the gnocchi among the four potato skins. To the same pan you used to sauté the gnocchi, add the remaining beer and reduce by half. Remove the beer from the heat and whisk in the remaining 3 tablespoons of butter. Finish each serving with a little lemon juice and garnish with a good pinch of grated Parmesan, 1 tablespoon sour cream, and 1 tablespoon of chives.

SWEETS & DESSERTS

ACTIVE PREP: 45 minutes
TOTAL TIME: 40–45 minutes (cake);
2 hours to overnight (ice cream)
SERVES: 6

DOPPELBOCK BUNDT CAKE

1 cup unsweetened natural cocoa powder
1 cup (8 fl oz/237 ml) doppelbock
1 cup (2 sticks) unsalted butter
½ cup packed brown sugar
2 cups flour
2 tsp baking soda
½ tsp baking powder
1 tsp salt
3 eggs
1 cup granulated sugar
¾ cup (6 fl oz/177 ml) buttermilk

DOPPELBOCK GANACHE

1 cup (8 fl oz/237 ml) heavy cream
½ cup (4 fl oz/118 ml) doppelbock
10 oz (283 g) quality bittersweet choco-
    late, pieces or chopped
½ tsp orange zest

DOPPELBOCK ICE CREAM

1 cup (8 fl oz/237 ml) heavy cream
½ cup (4 fl oz/118 ml) doppelbock
1 tsp orange zest
1 tsp pure vanilla extract
4 egg yolks
½ cup sugar

Paulaner Brauerei Salvator
(MUNICH, GERMANY)
Ayinger Celebrator
(AYING, GERMANY)

Doppelbock Buttermilk Bundt Cake with Ganache and Ice Cream

Preheat oven to 350°F (177°C). Prepare a Bundt cake pan by spraying it well with nonstick spray. Set aside.

Combine the cocoa powder, doppelbock, butter, and brown sugar in a saucepan over medium heat. Bring to a simmer stirring constantly. Be careful not to let the mixture boil over. When the butter is completely melted, remove from the heat and set aside to cool slightly.

Mix the flour, baking soda, baking powder, and salt together in a bowl. In a separate bowl, combine the eggs, granulated sugar, and buttermilk and mix on medium speed until well blended. Add the dry ingredients to the egg and sugar mixture and mix until just combined. Add the slightly cooled doppelbock mixture. Stir together until combined and uniform in color.

Pour the batter into the prepared Bundt pan. Do not fill the pan more than two-thirds full. Bake until just set, 40–45 minutes. Cool on a rack for 15 minutes. Turn out onto a plate and top with the Doppelbock Ganache.

While the cake bakes, make the ganache by heating the cream, doppelbock, and chocolate over medium heat to a simmer. Add the orange zest. Cook, stirring well to make sure the ganache is smooth and well-mixed, about 3 minutes. Remove from the heat and chill for at least an hour in the refrigerator before using.

Pour the ganache along the top of the cake, allowing the ganache to drip down the sides of the cake. Allow the cake to set for 30 minutes in the refrigerator before slicing and serving with Doppelbock Ice Cream.

Dopplebock Ice Cream

Combine the heavy cream, doppelbock, orange zest, and vanilla in a saucepan over medium heat and bring to a boil. Remove from the heat.

In a separate bowl, whisk together the egg yolks and the sugar. Add a couple of spoonfuls of the warm cream mixture to the eggs and sugar and stir. You need to warm up the eggs without scrambling them. Add another ¼ cup (2 fl oz/59 ml) of cream mixture to the eggs and stir.

Stir the egg and cream mixture into the remaining cream in the saucepan. Stir well. Return the pan to the heat and bring the mixture to a boil. Cook, stirring constantly, for another minute and then remove from the heat. Transfer the ice cream mixture to a cold bowl and chill for 20 minutes in the refrigerator.

Pour the chilled mixture into an ice cream maker and process according to the manufacturer's instructions. Place the ice cream in an airtight container and freeze for at least 2 hours. Serve with Doppelbock Buttermilk Bundt Cake.

ACTIVE PREP: 35 minutes
TOTAL TIME: 3 hours
SERVES: 12

LEMON CAKE

1 cup (2 sticks) unsalted butter at room
  temperature plus more for the Bundt
  cake pan

2½ cup sugar

3 cup all-purpose flour (plus more for the
  Bundt cake pan)

Zest of 1 lemon

1 tsp baking soda

1 tsp kosher salt

6 large eggs

½ cup (4 fl oz/118 ml) very hoppy beer

1 cup (8 fl oz/237 ml) sour cream

GOAT CHEESE-BEER ICING

1 cup powdered sugar

1 oz (28 g) goat cheese

2 Tbs (1 fl oz/30 ml) very hoppy beer

¼ cup (½ stick) butter, melted

For the lemon cake and icing, use the
freshest, hoppiest, imperial IPA available
to you.

Hoppy Lemon Bundt Cake with Goat Cheese-Beer Icing

Preheat oven to 350°F (177°C). Butter and flour a 12-cup (96 fl oz/2.8 l) Bundt pan.

With an electric stand mixer, beat the butter and sugar on high until light and fluffy. While your butter is whipping, combine the flour, lemon zest, baking soda, and salt; mix well.

Once the butter/sugar mixture is light and fluffy, add the eggs on low speed one at a time until fully incorporated. Alternately add the flour mixture, beer, and sour cream until it is fully incorporated.

Spoon the batter into the buttered and floured Bundt pan and tap the pan to even out the batter.

Bake 55–60 minutes or until a pick inserted into the center comes out clean. Remove from the oven and allow to cool for 15–20 minutes. Remove the cake from the pan to a cooling rack.

Once cool, top with goat cheese–beer icing and serve.

Goat Cheese-Beer Icing

In a medium mixing bowl, combine the sugar, goat cheese, and beer; mix well. Add the melted butter and whisk. Pour the icing over the cooled Bundt cake.

ACTIVE PREP: 20 minutes
TOTAL TIME: 55 minutes
SERVES: 12–16

MILK STOUT BROWNIES
1½ cup unbleached all-purpose flour
½ cup unsweetened cocoa powder
1 tsp instant coffee
½ tsp salt
3 large eggs
1½ cup sugar
1 tsp pure vanilla extract
½ cup (4 fl oz/118 ml) canola oil
½ cup (4 fl oz/118 ml) milk stout
4 Tbs (½ stick) unsalted butter, melted
8 oz (227 g) semisweet chocolate chips

COINTREAU WHIPPED CREAM
1 pint (16 fl oz/473 ml) heavy whipping
  cream
½ cup confectioner's sugar
1–2 Tbs (½–1 fl oz/15–30 ml) Cointreau
  or orange-flavored liqueur
Cocoa powder

Lefthand Brewing Milk Stout Nitro
(LONGMONT, COLORADO)
Brooklyn Brewery Black Chocolate Stout
(NEW YORK, NEW YORK)
Maui Brewing CoCoNut Porter
(KIHEI, HAWAII)

Milk Stout Brownies

Preheat oven to 350°F (176°C). Spray or grease a 9" × 13" (23 × 33 cm) baking pan.

Combine the flour, cocoa powder, coffee, and salt in a large bowl. Whisk the eggs, sugar, vanilla, and canola oil in a separate bowl. Add the dry ingredients to the egg mixture and stir well to combine. Mix in the milk stout and then the melted butter, stirring until just combined.

Stir in the chocolate chips. Do not overmix.

Pour the batter into the prepared pan and bake 30–35 minutes until brownies are slightly firm to the touch. Cool, cut, and enjoy with the Cointreau Whipped Cream.

Cointreau Whipped Cream
Chill the mixing bowl in the freezer for 10 minutes. Pour the heavy cream into the mixing bowl. Add the confectioner's sugar and liqueur. Using a stand or hand mixer, beat the mixture until stiff peaks are just about to form. Do not overbeat. Dollop on top of the Milk Stout Brownies and dust with the cocoa powder.

ACTIVE PREP: 30 minutes
TOTAL TIME: 2½ hours
SERVES: 4

BEER-GLAZED DONUTS

½ cup (4 fl oz/118 ml) warm water
¾ oz (21 g/3 packets) active dry yeast
2¼ cup (18 fl oz/532 ml) water
¾ cup sugar
1½ tsp salt
3 eggs
½ cup vegetable shortening
7½ cup all-purpose flour
Canola oil for frying

BEER GLAZE

½ cup (1 stick) butter, melted
3 cup powdered sugar
6–8 Tbs (3–4 fl oz/89–118 ml) of your
    favorite dark beer, room temperature

McEwans Scotch Ale
(EDINBURGH, SCOTLAND)
Lindemans Kriek Cuvée René
(VLEZENBEEK, BELGIUM)

Beer-Glazed Donuts

In a mixer, combine the warm water and yeast and let sit until the yeast blooms, about 5 minutes. Add the sugar, salt, eggs, shortening, and half of the flour. Mix on low until fully incorporated. Add the remaining flour and mix.

Remove the dough to a clean, dry mixing bowl, cover, and let rise until double in size. Move the dough to a floured work surface and use a rolling pin to roll to ½-inch (13 mm) thickness. Cut with a donut cutter.

Place the donuts on a cookie sheet, cover, and let rise for 30 more minutes.

Heat the oil to 325°F (163°C) in a tabletop fryer or a deep pot on the stove (use a candy thermometer). Fry the donuts until golden, flip, and fry on other side (about 45 seconds per side). Remove from the oil and allow to drain on a cooling rack. Glaze the donuts while they are still warm.

Beer Glaze

Combine all ingredients in a bowl and mix well. Drizzle the glaze over the warm donuts, then garnish with anything from crushed cookies to sprinkles.

ACTIVE PREP: 15 minutes
TOTAL TIME: 7½ hours (including refrigeration time)
SERVES: 10

1¾ cup cinnamon graham cracker crumbs (15–17 whole graham crackers)
3 Tbs light brown sugar
½ cup (1 stick) butter, melted
24 oz (680 g) cream cheese at room temperature
One 15 oz (425 g) can pumpkin puree
3 eggs plus 4 egg yolks
¼ cup (2 fl oz/59 ml) sour cream
1½ cup sugar
1 cup (8 fl oz/237 ml) pumpkin beer
4 Tbs all-purpose flour

Avery Brewing Rumpkin
(BOULDER, COLORADO)
Uinta Oak Jacked
(SALT LAKE CITY, UTAH)

Pumpkin-Beer Cheesecake

Preheat oven to 350°F (177°C).

In a medium bowl, combine the graham cracker crumbs, brown sugar, and melted butter. Mix until it resembles wet sand. Press into a 10-inch (25 cm) springform pan. Refrigerate while you assemble the batter.

Beat the cream cheese in an electric mixer until smooth. Add the pumpkin, eggs, egg yolks, sour cream, sugar, beer, and flour; mix well. Pour the batter into the chilled springform pan and bake 60–65 minutes. Remove from the oven and cool on a wire rack for 30 minutes. Cover and refrigerate at least 4–6 hours before serving.

ACTIVE PREP: 20 minutes
TOTAL TIME: 5–6 hours
MAKES: One 9-inch (23 cm) cheesecake

FILLING

2 lb (907 g) cream cheese (4 bricks),
  softened
1½ cup sugar
4 eggs
¾ cup (6 fl oz/177 ml) Pilsner
1 cup (8 fl oz/237 ml) sour cream
½ oz (14 g) basil chiffonade
1 tsp vanilla extract
¼ cup flour

CRUST

2½ cup graham cracker crumbs
1 Tbs sugar
3 Tbs butter, melted

STRAWBERRY PRESERVES

1 lb (454 g) strawberries, quartered
¼ cup sugar

Epic Hop Syndrome
(SALT LAKE CITY, UTAH)
Sixpoint Brewery The Crisp
(BROOKLYN, NEW YORK)
Left Hand Polestar Pilsner
(LONGMONT, COLORADO)

New York Basil-Beer Cheesecake with Strawberry Preserves

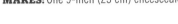

Filling

Preheat the oven to 350°F (177°C). With a stand or hand mixer, beat together the cream cheese and sugar until the mixture is smooth. Add the eggs one at a time, beating after each addition and scraping down the mixing bowl as needed. Stir in the remaining ingredients and mix until smooth. Allow the basil to steep while you prepare the crust.

Crust

Combine the graham cracker crumbs, sugar, and melted butter and mix well. Press the mixture onto the bottom of a 9" (23 cm) springform pan. Pour the cheesecake batter over the crust and bake for 50–60 minutes or until the center of the cheesecake is firm.

Turn off oven and allow the cheesecake to cool in the oven for 2–3 hours. Remove the cheesecake from the oven and refrigerate. To serve, place a slice of cheesecake on a plate and top with the strawberry preserves.

Strawberry Preserves

Combine the strawberries and sugar; mix well. Place the strawberry mixture into a mixing bowl and cover with plastic wrap. Place a pot of water on the stove and bring to a simmer. Place the mixing bowl directly on top of the simmering water and cook for 2–3 hours. Your syrup should be viscous enough to coat the back of a spoon.

Remove from the heat and cool.

ACTIVE PREP: 1 hour
TOTAL TIME: 10 hours
SERVES: 4–6

WAFFLES
2 cup flour
½ cup dried spent grain, ground
1 Tbs sugar
1 Tbs baking powder
1 tsp salt
3 eggs, whisked
1½ cup (12 fl oz/355 ml) milk
Juice and zest of 1 orange
½ lb (2 sticks) butter, melted

DOUBLE BOCK CARAMEL
2 cup sugar
1 Tbs butter at room temperature
½ cup (4 fl oz/118 ml) hot heavy cream
6 Tbs (3 fl oz/89 ml) double bock beer
2 oz (57 g) dark chocolate
½ tsp sea salt

BEER NUTS
2 cup sugar
2 cup (16 fl oz/473 ml) water
½ cup almonds, skin on
½ cup cashews
½ cup pecans
4 cup (32 fl oz/946 ml) vegetable oil
1 tsp sea salt

CHERRY-BEER MARASCHINOS
1 cup (8 fl oz/237 ml) cherry beer
1 cup maraschino cherries, preferably the good
  dark maraschino cherries such as Luxardo
  Maraschino Cherries

1 qt (32 fl oz/946 ml) ice cream
2 cup (16 fl oz/473 ml) whipped cream

Kulmbacher Eisbock
(KULMBACH, GERMANY)

Spent Grain Waffle Sundae with Chocolate Double Bock Caramel and Cherry-Beer Maraschinos

Waffles
In a medium bowl, combine the flour, spent grain, sugar, baking powder, and salt; mix well.

In a separate bowl, combine the eggs, milk, orange juice, and orange zest. Add the wet ingredients to the dry ingredients and mix well. Slowly add the melted butter to the batter and mix well.

Cook following the instructions with your waffle maker.

Double Bock Caramel
In a dry heavy-bottom pan, caramelize the sugar over medium-high heat. When the sugar is golden brown and fluid, add the butter and hot cream. Stir together over heat until it comes together.

Remove the pan from the heat and add the beer, chocolate, and salt; stir until combined.

Beer Nuts
In a medium saucepan, combine the sugar and water. Bring to a boil and add the nuts. Simmer for 2–3 minutes. Strain the mixture. Spread the nuts on a silicone mat or oiled parchment. Let dry completely (1–2 hours).

When the nuts are dry, heat the vegetable oil in a deep fryer. Fry the nuts for about 15 seconds and scoop out onto a rack to cool. Season with sea salt.

Cherry-Beer Maraschinos
In a wide-mouth jar with a screw lid, combine the cherry beer and the maraschino cherries. Refrigerate and let marinate overnight until they are delicious. Serve atop ice cream sundaes.

To serve, arrange 1–2 (depending on the size) waffles on a dessert plate. Top with a scoop of your favorite ice cream. Drizzle with Double Bock Caramel, sprinkle with nuts, and top with whipped cream and a Cherry-Beer Maraschino.

ACTIVE PREP: 35 minutes
TOTAL TIME: About 3 hours
SERVES: 6–8

1¼ cup sugar
3 Tbs all-purpose flour
Pinch salt
One (12 fl oz/357 ml) can evaporated milk
½ cup (4 fl oz/118 ml) Belgian golden
   strong ale
3 egg yolks
2 Tbs butter, cubed
1 tsp vanilla extract
1 box vanilla wafers (reserve 5 or 6 vani-
   alla wafers for crumbs for garnish)
3 bananas, sliced
1 cup (8 fl oz/237 ml) whipping cream,
   whipped

Deep Ellum Wealth and Taste
(DALLAS, TEXAS)
The Bruery Mischief
(PLACENTIA, CALIFORNIA)
Epic Brewing Brainless Golden Ale
(SALT LAKE CITY, UTAH)

Beer Banana Pudding

In a 3-quart (96 fl oz/2.8 l) heavy saucepan on low heat, combine the sugar, flour, and salt. Add the evaporated milk and beer and heat, stirring constantly, until the mixture begins to thicken, about 15 minutes.

Lightly beat the egg yolks in a medium bowl. Add a ladleful of the thickened milk mixture to the egg yolks and whisk. Return the egg mixture to the saucepan and continue to whisk and cook until incorporated, about 2 to 3 minutes. Remove the saucepan from the heat and stir in the butter and vanilla extract. Pour the custard into a bowl and cover with plastic wrap. Let cool in the refrigerator for 2½ hours.

In a large bowl or trifle dish, place a layer of half the vanilla wafers, a layer of half the sliced bananas, a layer of half the custard, and a layer of half the whipped cream. Repeat the layers. Crumble the reserved vanilla wafers and sprinkle the crumbs over the pudding.

ACTIVE PREP: 10 minutes
TOTAL TIME: 2 hours
SERVES: 3–4

1 cup (8 fl oz/237 ml) hoppy IPA
2½ cup (20 fl oz/591 ml) cold milk, divided
¼ cup (2 fl oz/59 ml) molasses
3 Tbs fine yellow cornmeal
1 egg
½ cup sugar
Pinch salt
½ tsp ginger, ground
½ tsp cinnamon, ground
3 Tbs butter

Southern Tier Right-o-Way
(LAKEWOOD, NEW YORK)
The Alchemist Heady Topper
(WATERBURY, VERMONT)
Lawsons Finest Liquids Sip Of Sunshine
(WARREN, VERMONT)

IPA Indian Pudding

Preheat the oven to 325°F (163°C). In a small saucepan, combine the beer and 2 cup (16 fl oz/473 ml) milk and bring to a boil. Reduce heat to medium-low and add molasses and the cornmeal. Cook until it thickens.

In a separate bowl, combine the egg, sugar, salt, ginger, and cinnamon. Add the cornmeal mixture and mix well. Stir in the butter and remaining ½ cup (4 fl oz/118 ml) cold milk. Bake for 90 minutes.

Once cooled, the pudding should be soft but set.

Serve with ice cream.

ACTIVE PREP: 20 minutes
TOTAL TIME: 80 minutes
SERVES: 4

1½ cup (12 fl oz/355 ml) pumpkin puree
  (canned is fine)

½ cup brown sugar

½ cup white sugar

½ tsp ground ginger

½ tsp ground cinnamon

¼ tsp ground nutmeg

½ tsp kosher salt

1 cup (8 fl oz/237 ml) sour cream

3 cup (24 fl oz/710 ml) heavy whipping
  cream, divided

16 Italian ladyfinger cookies (savoiardi),
  halved crosswise

½ cup (4 fl oz/118 ml) Belgian-style quad

4 oz (113 g) dark chocolate, chopped,
  ground on a microplane, or shredded on
  a box grater.

Avery The Reverend
(BOULDER, COLORADO)
Straffe Hendrik Quad
(BRUGGE, BELGIUM)
Elevation Apis IV Honey Quadrupel
(PONCHA SPRINGS, COLORADO)

Pumpkin Mousse Tiramisu with Quad Soaked Lady Fingers and Shaved Chocolate

In a large bowl, combine the pumpkin, brown sugar, sugar, ginger, cinnamon, nutmeg, salt, sour cream, and 2 cups (16 fl oz/473 ml) of the heavy cream. Using either a tabletop or hand mixer, beat on medium speed until soft peaks form.

In a separate bowl, beat the remaining cup (8 fl oz/237 ml) of whipping cream to stiff peaks.

In 4 tulip glasses, begin to assemble the tiramisu with ¼ cup (2 fl oz/59 ml) of the pumpkin mousse in the bottom of each glass. For each glass, dip 4 ladyfinger halves in the beer quickly and place on the mousse, top with a thin layer of chocolate. Repeat the layers, ending with the chocolate. Top with the whipped cream and garnish with a little of the chocolate. Allow to set in the refrigerator for 1 hour before serving.

ACTIVE PREP: 20 minutes
TOTAL TIME: 65 minutes
SERVES: 6

FRUIT FILLING

4 cup mixed summer berries (raspberries, blueberries, quartered strawberries, blackberries)
1 Tbs cornstarch
2 Tbs (1 fl oz/30 ml) bourbon-barrel-aged stout
¼ cup sugar
½ tsp ground cinnamon
½ tsp ground ginger
Pinch of salt

CRUMBLE

½ cup flour
1 cup rolled oats (not quick cooking)
½ cup brown sugar
½ tsp cinnamon
¼ tsp salt
6 Tbs butter, cut into small pieces
½ cup chopped pecans (optional)

SAUCE

1½ cup (12 fl oz/355 ml) bourbon-barrel-aged stout
2 Tbs brown sugar
1 Tbs butter

Goose Island Bourbon County Brand Stout
(CHICAGO, ILLINOIS)
Elevation Beer Co. Oil Man Stout
(PONCHA SPRINGS, COLORADO)
The Bruery Black Tuesday
(PLACENTIA, CALIFORNIA)

Bourbon-Barrel-Aged Stout Fruit Crumble

Heat oven to 375°F (190°C). Wash the fruit and place it in a mixing bowl. Add the cornstarch, beer, sugar, spices, and salt, and stir to coat. Pour the fruit filling into an 8" × 8" (20 cm × 20 cm) baking dish.

Combine the flour, oats, brown sugar, cinnamon, and salt in a mixing bowl. Add the butter chunks and knead butter into dry ingredients until it comes together in clumps. Fold the nuts into the mixture.

Crumble the topping over the fruit, evenly distributing it across the dish. Bake for 45–50 minutes until nicely browned and bubbly. Cool slightly.

Pour the beer into a medium saucepan. Add the sugar and stir to combine. Over medium heat, bring to a simmer and cook, stirring to reduce the liquid by half. Remove from the heat, add the butter, stirring until it melts. Cool slightly.

Serve the crumble warm with ice cream and sauce.

ACTIVE PREP: 35 minutes
TOTAL TIME: 2¼ hours
SERVES: 4

1 cup sugar
½ cup all-purpose flour
½ cup (4 fl oz /118 ml) cup porter
1½ cup (12 fl oz/355 ml) heavy cream
1 vanilla bean, scraped
1 prebaked pie shell
1 piece whole nutmeg

Southern Tier Porter
(LAKEWOOD, NEW YORK)
Breckenridge Brewery Vanilla Porter
(DENVER, COLORADO)

Porter Sugar Cream Pie

Preheat the oven to 375°F (191°C). In a medium bowl, stir together the sugar and flour.

In a separate bowl, combine the beer, cream, and vanilla bean. Stir the wet ingredients into the dry ingredients and mix gently but well. Pour the batter into the pie shell and bake on the center rack for 90 minutes. Make sure the pie jiggles a little when you tap the side.

Remove from the oven and allow to cool. Top the pie with a light grating of nutmeg.

ACTIVE PREP: 20 minutes
TOTAL TIME: 6–8 hours to allow the ice cream to freeze
SERVES: 4

**BUTTER CARAMEL,
SALTED PEANUT ICE CREAM**
Makes: 2 quart (64 fl oz/1.9 l)

2½ cup (20 fl oz/592 ml) milk
3 cup (24 fl oz/710 ml) cream
½ cup (4 fl oz/118 ml) IPA
8 egg yolks
3 cup sugar
6 Tbs butter, chilled
1 Tbs kosher salt
1 cup roasted and salted peanuts,
  crushed

PAIN PERDU
¾ cup (6 fl oz/177 ml) milk
¼ cup (2 fl oz/59 ml) IPA
2 Tbs cocoa powder
¾ cup powdered sugar
4 eggs
4 Tbs butter
8 slices white, sourdough, or other favorite bread, left out overnight
Butter Caramel-Salted Peanut Ice Cream

Firestone Walker Easy Jack
(PASO ROBLES, CALIFORNIA)
New Belgium Slow Ride
(FORT COLLINS, COLORADO)
Harpoon Take 5
(BOSTON, MASSACHUSETTS)

Chocolate Pain Perdu with Butter Caramel, Salted Peanut Ice Cream

Butter Caramel, Salted Peanut Ice Cream

In a medium saucepan, combine the milk, cream, and beer. Scald the mixture by heating on medium-low, stirring frequently, until small bubbles begin to form around the edges. Remove the pan from the heat.

In a mixing bowl, combine the egg yolks and 1 cup of the sugar. Pour one-third of the hot milk mixture into the egg yolk mixture and stir briskly. Return the egg and cream mixture to the saucepan and cook over medium heat until the mixture thickens enough to coat a spoon. Remove from the heat.

Place the remaining 2 cups of sugar and the salt in another heavy-bottom pan over medium heat. Stirring from the outside in, cook until the sugar begins to melt. When there is only a little sugar left, remove the pan from the heat and stir in the butter, 2 tablespoons at a time. Once the butter is incorporated, pour the warm ice cream custard over the caramel and stir until the caramel is fully incorporated. Chill.

Using your ice cream maker's specific directions, freeze the custard until ribbons form on top. Fold in the peanuts and freeze fully.

Pain Perdu

In a small saucepan, combine the milk, beer, cocoa powder, and sugar and mix well. Warm over low heat just until the cocoa powder and sugar dissolve. In a pie plate or shallow dish, whisk the eggs. Slowly whisk in the warmed milk mixture until fully combined.

On a griddle or large pan over medium heat, melt 1–2 tablespoon of butter. Dip the bread slices in the batter and allow to soak for a minute. Cook the pain perdu slices on the griddle until brown on both sides. Remove to a plate and keep warm. Add more butter to the griddle, if needed, and cook the remaining pain perdu slices.

To serve, place two pain perdu slices on each plate and top with one scoop of Butter Caramel-Salted Peanut Ice Cream.

ACTIVE PREP: 45 minutes

TOTAL TIME: 9 hours (including time to let the marshmallows set)

SERVES: 6–10

PORTER MARSHMALLOWS

1½ cup (12 fl oz/355 ml) porter
2 Tbs granulated sugar
Three ¼ oz (7 g) gelatin packets
2 Tbs (1 fl oz/30 ml) canola oil
2 cup powdered sugar

GANACHE

½ cup (4 fl oz/118 ml) heavy cream
8 oz (227 g) semisweet chocolate, chopped into small pieces

1 box graham crackers

Ballast Point Victory at Sea Porter
(SAN DIEGO, CALIFORNIA)

Beer S'Mores with Porter Marshmallows and Ganache

Porter Marshmallows

Combine the porter and granulated sugar in a medium sauce pan over medium-high heat. Simmer for 5 minutes. Remove from the heat and allow to cool to 80°F (27°C).

Pour the beer/sugar mixture into the bowl of a stand mixer and add the 3 gelatin packs. Let stand for 7 minutes. Using a whisk, mix on high speed until the beer quadruples in volume and starts to show signs of soft peaks.

While the mixer is going, lightly coat a 6" × 9" (15 cm × 23 cm) pan with the canola oil. Pour the marshmallow mixture into the oiled pan, cover, and refrigerate to set overnight.

Remove from the refrigerator and portion the marshmallows into 1½-inch (4 cm) squares. Cut with a hot knife.

Remove from the pan and toss in the powdered sugar till coated.

Ganache

Combine the chocolate and cream in a metal mixing bowl. Place the bowl over a pot of boiling water and stir until the chocolate is smooth.

Break the graham crackers into squares to fit your marshmallows. Place a dollop of ganache on 1 graham cracker. Place the marshmallow on top of the ganache. Top the marshmallow with 1 tablespoon (15 ml) of the ganache. Place the second graham cracker on top and finish with another tablespoon of ganache. Repeat until you have used all your marshmallows.

Index

A

Aged Gouda & Beer Soup 84
Andouille Sausage 120

B

Baby Back Ribs 116
Bacon 22, 40, 54, 124
Beer Batter 38, 100
Beer Style
    Amber 16, 48, 88
    American Lager 100
    Belgian Golden Strong Ale 58, 144
    Belgian-style Quadrupel 148
    Belgian-style Wit 24, 64, 112
    Blonde Ale 92
    Bock 14, 142
    Bourbon-Barrel-Aged Stout 150
    Brown Ale 8, 38, 66, 80, 86
    Doppelbock 46, 130, 142
    English mild 42
    ESB 32
    Golden Sour 72
    Gruit 60
    Gueuze 52
    Hard Cider 118
    Imperial Stout 108
    IPA 18, 20, 28, 34, 50, 62, 68, 78, 82, 102, 110,
        132, 146, 154
    Lager 10, 38, 40, 48, 122
    Lambic 52
    Maibock 14, 114
    Märzen 94, 106
    Milk Stout 134
    Pale Ale 12, 54
    Pilsner 12, 24, 26, 100, 126, 140
    Porter 22, 104, 114, 116, 134, 152, 156
    Pumpkin Beer 138
    Saison 16, 76, 98
    Sour Beer 30, 36
    Stout 22, 108, 120, 134, 150
    Tripel 34, 84
    Vienna Lager 40, 48
    Wheat Beer 96, 124
    White Ale 112
Beer-Tomato Broth 16
Biscuit 24
Blue Cheese Beer Butter 102
Brewery
    10 Barrel 62
    Achel 70
    Aecht Schlenkerla 124
    Against the Grain 66
    Alaskan 22, 88
    Allagash 24, 74, 84, 94
    Anchor 104
    Angry Orchard 118

August Schell 12, 48, 100
Avery Brewing 8, 138
Ayinger Brewery 14, 46, 126, 130
Ballast Point 12, 16, 82, 156
Barley Brown's 62
Bell's 96, 110
Big Sky 38
Boon 52
Boulevard 16, 98
Brasserie Dupont 16, 98
Breckenridge 152
Brooklyn Brewery 134
Brouwerij Bosteels 64, 84, 94
Brouwerij Huyghe 58
Chimay 64
Crooked Stave 10, 52
Deep Ellum 144
Deschutes 22, 104, 116, 118
Devils Backbone 40, 48
Dogfish Head 8, 110
Elevation 148, 150
Epic Brewing 14, 46, 80, 108, 126, 140, 144
Firestone Walker 20, 26, 34, 54, 72, 98,
    102, 154
Fort Collins Brewery 14, 114
Founders 60, 78, 104, 108, 112
Funkwerks 98
Goose Island 108, 150
Great Lakes 18, 40, 106
Green Man 32
Guinness 100
Harpoon 154
High Hops 120
Humboldt 82, 86
Jack's Abby 46, 112
Jester King 78
Kona Brewing 116
Kulmbacher 142
Lagunitas 102
Lawsons Finest Liquids 146
Left Hand 18, 32, 134, 140
Lindemans 72, 136
Live Oak 26, 48
Mad River 120
MadTree 80
Maui Brewing 134
McEwans 136
Modern Times 96
Neshaminy Creek 106
New Belgium 16, 30, 60, 72, 74, 84, 88, 118,
    126, 154
New Glarus 100
Newport Storm 22
Odell Brewing 20, 54, 78, 88, 102, 116
Ommegang 34, 92
Paulaner Brauerei 130
Pilsner Urquell 24
Port Brewing 66

Prairie Artisan Ales 10
Rodenbach 30
Samuel Adams 38, 40
Samuel Smith's 18
Schlafly 102
Schneider Weiss 124
Sierra Nevada 114
Sixpoint 12, 140
Ska Brewing 92, 112
Smuttynose 64
Southern Tier 56, 114, 146, 152
St. Bernardus 74
Stone 76, 118
Straffe Hendrik 148
Straight to Ale 68
Summit Brewing 42
Surly Brewing 8, 38, 106
Sweetwater 114
Tallgrass 120
The Alchemist 146
The Bruery 10, 36, 58, 122, 144, 150
The Lost Abbey 56, 70
The Rare Barrel 30, 52
Thirsty Dog 28
Uinta 50, 66, 76, 138
Union Craft Beer 50
Upslope 86
Victory Brewing 10, 12, 94, 102, 122
Weihenstephaner 10
Westmalle 70
Wicked Weed 68
Yards 18
Brisket 104
Brownies 134
Bundt Cake 130, 132

C

Ceviche 10
Cheddar Dijon 24
Cheese
    Blue Cheese 28, 62, 102
    Cheddar 24, 54
    Comté 86
    Fontina 58
    Goat Cheese 12, 46, 52, 74, 132
    Gouda 64, 84
    Ricotta 16
Cheesecake 138, 140
Cheese Sauce 58
Chicken 28, 110, 112
Chicken Wings 28
Chile Rellenos 52
Chorizo 98
Clams 22
Cod 98
Corn & Beer Soup 88
Cornbread 124

Crab Cakes 50
Crab Salad 88

D

Donuts 136
Duck Breast 46

F

Fish Fry 100
Flatbread 74
French Onion Soup 86
Fritters 40
Frogmore Stew 78
Fruit
    Apple-Fennel Slaw 92
    Banana Pudding 144
    Fig 46
    Fruit Crumble 150
    Maraschinos 142
    Pumpkin 138, 148
    Winter Melon Pickle 122

G

Giardiniera Relish 76
Glazes & Icings
    Beer Glaze 136
    Chocolate Ganache 156
    Doppelbock Ganache 130
    Double Bock Caramel 142
    Goat Cheese-Beer Icing 132
Gnocchi 126

H

Ham 118
Herb-Marinated Goat Cheese 12
Hush Puppies 32

I

Ice Cream
    Butter Caramel, Salted Peanut 154
    Dopplebock 130
Indian Pudding 146
IPA-Brined Veggie Relish 68
Italian-style Beef 76

K

Kentucky Hot Brown 66

L

Lamb 16, 70
Legume
    Pinto Beans 124

M

Marshmallows 156
Michelada Chicken 112
Muffaletta 68
Mussels 94, 96, 98

O

Oysters 14, 30

P

Pain Perdu 154
Panzanella 46, 64
Pesto 60
Pickled Onions 24
Pistachio 70
Polenta 56
Pork Belly 20
Pork Ribs 122
Porter Brine 104
Porter Sugar Cream Pie 152
Portobello Fries 38
Posole 82
Potato Skins 42, 126
Pot Pie 106
Pudding 144, 146

Q

Quail 114
Quiche 54
    Crust (Pâte Brisée) 54
    Filling 54

R

Rib-Eye Steak 102
Roast Beef 108
Rueben Chowder 80

S

Salad 46, 60, 62, 70, 88, 92
Salad Dressings
    Blue Cheese Vinaigrette 62
    Creamy Dressing 64
    Doppelbock-Fig Dressing 46
    Gruit Pesto Dressing 60
    Maibock Vinaigrette 114
Salami 64
Salmon 8, 92
Sauces
    Apricot IPA Sauce 110
    Beer Butter Sauce 98
    Beer Caramel 122
    Blue Cheese Dipping Sauce 28

    Crème Fraiche 42
    Curried Mayo Sauce 18
    Double Bock Caramel 142
    Gribiche Sauce 38
    Hitachino Sweet Sauce 112
    Hops Bearnaise 92
    Horseradish Crema 8
    Mignonette Sauce 30
    Mornay Sauce 66
    Red Chile Purée 82
Sausage 24, 78, 120
Scallops 94
Short Ribs 76, 106
Shrimp 10, 18, 26, 78
Smoky Links 96
Smoky Mussel Märzen Broth 94
S'Mores 156
Sour Beer Lobster Rolls 72
Spaetzle 58
Sriracha 14, 28
Striped Bass 48
Sugar Cream Pie 152

T

Tiramisu 148
Toasted Capers 8
Tostadas 48
Trout 74

V

Vegetable
    Beer-Braised Mushrooms 56
    Broccoli 62, 108
    Brussel Sprouts 94
    Capers 8
    Caramelized Sweet Potatoes 46
    Cauliflower-Bacon Fritters 40
    Cinnamon Truffle Squash Puree 104
    Fennel 64, 92
    French Onion Soup 86
    IPA-Brined Veggie Relish 68
    Kale 96
    Sour Beer Pickled Vegetables 36
    Spicy Belgian Ale Brussels 34
    Squash 104
    Sweet Potato 46
    Tomatillo Salsa 48

W

Waffle 8, 142
Wheat-Beer Broth 96